ASYLEES

Rob Staeger

THE CHANGING
Face of North America:
IMMIGRATION SINCE 1965

ASYLEES

Rob Staeger

MASON CREST PUBLISHERS
PHILADELPHIA

Produced by OTTN Publishing, Stockton, New Jersey

Mason Crest Publishers
370 Reed Road
Broomall, PA 19008
www.masoncrest.com

First printing

1 3 5 7 9 8 6 4 2

Library of Congress Cataloging-in-Publication Data

Staeger, Rob.
  Asylees / Rob Staeger.
    p. cm. — (The changing face of North America)
Summary: Discusses the asylum process, differences between asylees and refugees, specific asylum cases, and changes in the laws since the 1960s and particularly since September 11, 2001.
Includes bibliographical references and index.
  ISBN 1-59084-685-0
1. Refugees—United States—Juvenile literature. 2. Asylum, Right of—United States—Juvenile literature.
[1. Refugees. 2. Asylum, Right of.] I. Title. II. Series.
JV6601.S73 2004
323.6'31—dc22
                                                        2003018381

THE CHANGING Face of North America:
IMMIGRATION SINCE 1965

CONTENTS

INTRODUCTION

THE CHANGING FACE OF AMERICA

By Senator Edward M. Kennedy

America is proud of its heritage and history as a nation of immigrants, and my own family is an example. All eight of my great-grandparents were immigrants who left Ireland a century and a half ago, when that land was devastated by the massive famine caused by the potato blight. When I was a young boy, my grandfather used to take me down to the docks in Boston and regale me with stories about the Great Famine and the waves of Irish immigrants who came to America seeking a better life. He talked of how the Irish left their marks in Boston and across the nation, enduring many hardships and harsh discrimination, but also building the railroads, digging the canals, settling the West, and filling the factories of a growing America. According to one well-known saying of the time, "under every railroad tie, an Irishman is buried."

America was the promised land for them, as it has been for so many other immigrants who have found shelter, hope, opportunity, and freedom. Immigrants have always been an indispensable part of our nation. They have contributed immensely to our communities, created new jobs and whole new industries, served in our armed forces, and helped make America the continuing land of promise that it is today.

The inspiring poem by Emma Lazarus, inscribed on the pedestal of the Statue of Liberty in New York Harbor, is America's welcome to all immigrants:

Give me your tired, your poor,
Your huddled masses yearning to breathe free,
The wretched refuse of your teeming shore,
Send these, the homeless, tempest-tossed, to me:
I lift my lamp beside the golden door.

The period since September 11, 2001, has been particularly challenging for immigrants. Since the horrifying terrorist attacks, there has been a resurgence of anti-immigrant attitudes and behavior. We all agree that our borders must be safe and secure. Yet, at the same time, we must safeguard the entry of the millions of persons who come to the United States legally each year as immigrants, visitors, scholars, students, and workers. The "golden door" must stay open. We must recognize that immigration is not the problem—terrorism is. We must identify and isolate the terrorists, and not isolate America.

One of my most important responsibilities in the Senate is the preservation of basic rights and basic fairness in the application of our immigration laws, so that new generations of immigrants in our own time and for all time will have the same opportunity that my great-grandparents had when they arrived in America.

Immigration is beneficial for the United States and for countries throughout the world. It is no coincidence that two hundred years ago, our nations' founders chose *E Pluribus Unum*—"out of many, one"—as America's motto. These words, chosen by Benjamin Franklin, John Adams, and Thomas Jefferson, refer to the ideal that separate colonies can be transformed into one united nation. Today, this ideal has come to apply to individuals as well. Our diversity is our strength. We are a nation of immigrants, and we always will be.

THE CHANGING FACE OF THE UNITED STATES

Marian L. Smith, historian
U.S. Immigration and Naturalization Service

Americans commonly assume that immigration today is very different than immigration of the past. The immigrants themselves appear to be unlike immigrants of earlier eras. Their language, their dress, their food, and their ways seem strange. At times people fear too many of these new immigrants will destroy the America they know. But has anything really changed? Do new immigrants have any different effect on America than old immigrants a century ago? Is the American fear of too much immigration a new development? Do immigrants really change America more than America changes the immigrants? The very subject of immigration raises many questions.

In the United States, immigration is more than a chapter in a history book. It is a continuous thread that links the present moment to the first settlers on North American shores. From the first colonists' arrival until today, immigrants have been met by Americans who both welcomed and feared them. Immigrant contributions were always welcome—on the farm, in the fields, and in the factories. Welcoming the poor, the persecuted, and the "huddled masses" became an American principle. Beginning with the original Pilgrims' flight from religious persecution in the 1600s, through the Irish migration to escape starvation in the 1800s, to the relocation of Central Americans seeking refuge from civil wars in the 1980s and 1990s, the United States has considered itself a haven for the destitute and the oppressed.

But there was also concern that immigrants would not adopt American ways, habits, or language. Too many immigrants might overwhelm America. If so, the dream of the Founding Fathers for United States government and society would be destroyed. For this reason, throughout American history some have argued that limiting or ending immigration is our patriotic duty. Benjamin Franklin feared there were so many German immigrants in Pennsylvania the Colonial Legislature would begin speaking German. "Progressive" leaders of the early 1900s feared that immigrants who could not read and understand the English language were not only exploited by "big business," but also served as the foundation for "machine politics" that undermined the U.S. Constitution. This theme continues today, usually voiced by those who bear no malice toward immigrants but who want to preserve American ideals.

Have immigrants changed? In colonial days, when most colonists were of English descent, they considered Germans, Swiss, and French immigrants as different. They were not "one of us" because they spoke a different language. Generations later, Americans of German or French descent viewed Polish, Italian, and Russian immigrants as strange. They were not "like us" because they had a different religion, or because they did not come from a tradition of constitutional government. Recently, Americans of Polish or Italian descent have seen Nicaraguan, Pakistani, or Vietnamese immigrants as too different to be included. It has long been said of American immigration that the latest ones to arrive usually want to close the door behind them.

It is important to remember that fear of individual immigrant groups seldom lasted, and always lessened. Benjamin Franklin's anxiety over German immigrants disappeared after those immigrants' sons and daughters helped the nation gain independence in the Revolutionary War. The Irish of the mid-1800s were among the most hated immigrants, but today we all wear green on St. Patrick's Day. While a century ago it was feared that Italian and other Catholic immigrants would vote as directed by the Pope, today that controversy is only a vague memory. Unfortunately, some ethnic groups continue their efforts to earn acceptance. The African

Americans' struggle continues, and some Asian Americans, whose families have been in America for generations, are the victims of current anti-immigrant sentiment.

Time changes both immigrants and America. Each wave of new immigrants, with their strange language and habits, eventually grows old and passes away. Their American-born children speak English. The immigrants' grandchildren are completely American. The strange foods of their ancestors—spaghetti, baklava, hummus, or tofu—become common in any American restaurant or grocery store. Much of what the immigrants brought to these shores is lost, principally their language. And what is gained becomes as American as St. Patrick's Day, Hanukkah, or Cinco de Mayo, and we forget that it was once something foreign.

Recent immigrants are all around us. They come from every corner of the earth to join in the American Dream. They will continue to help make the American Dream a reality, just as all the immigrants who came before them have done.

FOREWORD

THE CHANGING FACE OF CANADA

Peter A. Hammerschmidt
First Secretary, Permanent Mission of Canada to the United Nations

Throughout Canada's history, immigration has shaped and defined the very character of Canadian society. The migration of peoples from every part of the world into Canada has profoundly changed the way we look, speak, eat, and live. Through close and distant relatives who left their lands in search of a better life, all Canadians have links to immigrant pasts. We are a nation built by and of immigrants.

Two parallel forces have shaped the history of Canadian immigration. The enormous diversity of Canada's immigrant population is the most obvious. In the beginning came the enterprising settlers of the "New World," the French and English colonists. Soon after came the Scottish, Irish, and Northern and Central European farmers of the 1700s and 1800s. As the country expanded westward during the mid-1800s, migrant workers began arriving from China, Japan, and other Asian countries. And the turbulent twentieth century brought an even greater variety of immigrants to Canada, from the Caribbean, Africa, India, and Southeast Asia.

So while English- and French-Canadians are the largest ethnic groups in the country today, neither group alone represents a majority of the population. A large and vibrant multicultural mix makes up the rest, particularly in Canada's major cities. Toronto, Vancouver, and Montreal alone are home to people from over 200 ethnic groups!

Less obvious but equally important in the evolution of Canadian immigration has been hope. The promise of a better life lured Europeans and Americans seeking cheap (sometimes even free) farmland. Thousands of Scots and Irish arrived to escape grinding poverty and starvation. Others came for freedom, to escape religious and political persecution. Canada has long been a haven to the world's dispossessed and disenfranchised—Dutch and German farmers cast out for their religious beliefs, black slaves fleeing the United States, and political refugees of despotic regimes in Europe, Africa, Asia, and South America.

The two forces of diversity and hope, so central to Canada's past, also shaped the modern era of Canadian immigration. Following the Second World War, Canada drew heavily on these influences to forge trailblazing immigration initiatives.

The catalyst for change was the adoption of the Canadian Bill of Rights in 1960. Recognizing its growing diversity and Canadians' changing attitudes towards racism, the government passed a federal statute barring discrimination on the grounds of race, national origin, color, religion, or sex. Effectively rejecting the discriminatory elements in Canadian immigration policy, the Bill of Rights forced the introduction of a new policy in 1962. The focus of immigration abruptly switched from national origin to the individual's potential contribution to Canadian society. The door to Canada was now open to every corner of the world.

Welcoming those seeking new hopes in a new land has also been a feature of Canadian immigration in the modern era. The focus on economic immigration has increased along with Canada's steadily growing economy, but political immigration has also been encouraged. Since 1945, Canada has admitted tens of thousands of displaced persons, including Jewish Holocaust survivors, victims of Soviet crackdowns in Hungary and Czechoslovakia, and refugees from political upheaval in Uganda, Chile, and Vietnam.

Prior to 1978, however, these political refugees were admitted as an exception to normal immigration procedures. That year, Canada revamped its refugee policy with a new Immigration Act that explicitly affirmed Canada's commitment to the resettlement of refugees from oppression. Today, the admission of refugees remains a central part of Canadian immigration law and regulations.

Amendments to economic and political immigration policy continued during the 1980s and 1990s, refining further the bold steps taken during the modern era. Together, these initiatives have turned Canada into one of the world's few truly multicultural states.

Unlike the process of assimilation into a "melting pot" of cultures, immigrants to Canada are more likely to retain their cultural identity, beliefs, and practices. This is the source of some of Canada's greatest strengths as a society. And as a truly multicultural nation, diversity is not seen as a threat to Canadian identity. Quite the contrary—diversity *is* Canadian identity.

1 WHAT IS AN ASYLEE?

A tank rolled down the street. Vesna, a Bosnian teenager, watched from behind the curtains of her bedroom window. The tank rolled past her house and out of sight. A few minutes later, she heard an explosion. She later found out which homes of her neighbors were no longer standing.

Daily life was terrifying in Sarajevo, the shell-shocked capital of Bosnia and Herzegovina, which is formerly a region of Yugoslavia. Serbians bombed the city every day. Vesna's parents worked long hours in the hospital, tending to the injured and the sick. As if the tanks weren't bad enough, there were reports of violence in other towns and neighborhoods. Soldiers were killing people. Horrible crimes were being committed against women. Vesna's parents agreed: she had to leave the country to be safe. They made arrangements for her to go to the airport.

Vesna's brother was not able to come with her. He had been drafted into the army, and had to stay and fight the Serbs. Her sister Maja and Maja's husband would stay behind as well. But Maja, who had gone to France a few years before, gave Vesna her passport. Maja was six years older, but looked enough like Vesna in her photo. It might get her through airport security.

Vesna's parents bought plane tickets with money they had saved. More money went to bribe an official at the airport. He could get her on a plane to Slovenia. From there, she would fly to Paris and connect with a flight to New York.

◀ The bombed ruins of buses and buildings in Sarajevo, the capital of Bosnia and Herzegovina, 1996. The former Yugoslavia is one of many regions that in recent decades have produced victims looking for asylum in the United States and Canada.

By the time Vesna reached her third flight, exhaustion had taken over. She slept most of the trip, but when the pilot announced the plane's approach to New York, all weariness fled her. In its place was anxiety mixed with relief. She had finally escaped the dangers of Bosnia. But would the U.S. authorities let her in? If she made it through customs, how would she live? And would she ever see her family again?

The plane landed in John F. Kennedy Airport. Passengers left the plane and lined up for U.S. Immigration. Vesna took her place in line. She nervously fingered her sister's passport. Would it be good enough to get her through?

The inspector eyed the passport closely. Then he directed Vesna to one of a dozen small rooms connected to the larger waiting room. Another officer entered and questioned her closely. He said she didn't look like she was 23. He asked Vesna where she went in France. She tried to remember what she could from Maja's photo albums.

As Vesna spoke, she knew the officer thought she was lying. She had only once option—to tell the truth. "Those are my sister's papers. My name is Vesna, and I need asylum," she said. With these words, Vesna entered the U.S. asylum system.

Victims of a shelling attack in Sarajevo lie in a morgue, 1994. One reason why asylees may not want to return to their home country is that they face the direct threat of violence or war there.

Asylees and Refugees

Vesna is not a real person; the above story is only a composite of asylum accounts. However, the details of her journey are very typical of Bosnian asylees, as well as those from other troubled parts of the world. Anyone who receives asylum in the United States is called an *asylee*. In popular usage, an asylee is a type of *refugee*, who is defined as any person who is driven from his or her country because of persecution. However, under U.S. law, there is an important distinction between refugees and asylees, which depends on their location when they are processed. Those processed *within* the United States and who meet the legal definition are asylees; those who are processed *outside* the United States and meet the definition are refugees.

When it is decided that asylees meet the proper definition, they are granted asylum and allowed to remain in the host country. They continue to be referred to as asylees rather than refugees, though the only distinction is their location when they were first processed.

Along with many other countries, the United States has signed the 1967 Protocol Relating to the Status of Refugees, an agreement drawn up by the United Nations that promises rights to refugees. The most important of these rights is called non-refoulement. Refoulement is the forced return of refugees to their countries of origin.

What Is a Refugee?

The 1967 Protocol also establishes detailed criteria for a refugee. According to the document, a refugee is "a person outside of his or her country of nationality who is unable or unwilling to return because of persecution or a well-founded fear of persecution on account of race, religion, nationality, membership in a particular social group, or political opinion."

It's a complex definition, but it is important that it be that specific. The definition sets the standard by which a person is a refugee, and the U.S. government applies this standard to judge asylum cases. To best understand the definition, it helps to examine it step by step:

The first phrase, "outside of his or her country of nationality," simply means someone who has left his or her home country. Those who have left their homes, but not their country, are not refugees; they are called "internally displaced people."

The next phrase presents the condition of the person being "unable or unwilling to return" to the home country. This covers two different situations. In the first, an individual won't return home because he or she fears the government of the home country. Most refugees have this fear. Often, they leave

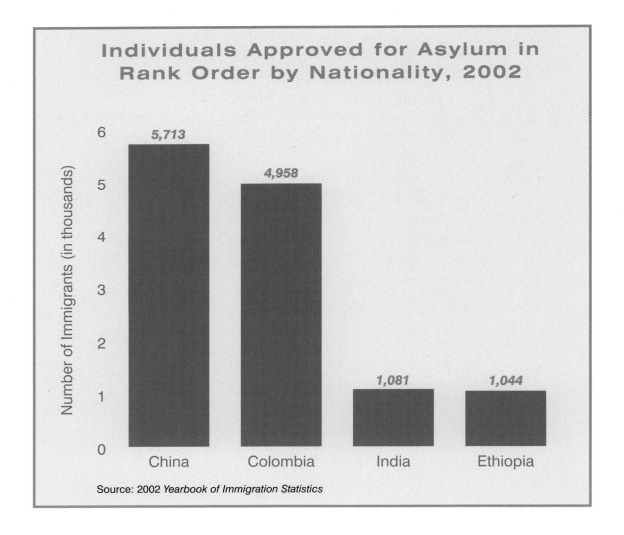

Source: 2002 *Yearbook of Immigration Statistics*

their country because their government is harming them through violence or intimidation.

In the second case, an individual leaves to avoid another group or event against which the government can't offer protection. The threat may come from a rebel group that opposes the government, or a powerful religious group that persecutes others. The government may be afraid of or sympathetic to the group, and so it allows the group to do as it pleases, even if it is committing or threatening to commit violence against innocent citizens.

The third and most important part of the definition is the section about persecution. A refugee must have either experienced persecution firsthand or have a "well-founded fear" of persecution were he or she to return to the home country. It is important to recognize that persecution has as much to do with the victim as the persecutor. Unlike random mistreatment or harm, persecution is more personal in nature: people who are persecuted are singled out for who they are, what they say, or what groups they belong to. The refugee definition lays out five grounds of persecution: race, religion, nationality, membership in a social group, and political opinion. Only persecution under these grounds can qualify people as refugees.

Grounds of Persecution

The first three grounds of persecution are fairly self-explanatory. Racial differences are easy to identify, and minority races often make convenient scapegoats for failed governments. Religious minorities, like ethnic minorities, have been persecuted throughout history. Even powerless *majorities*—such as the black South Africans during the Apartheid era of the 20th century—can be victims of persecution.

Political opinion is often less a result of someone's background than his or her beliefs. Many times individuals will be targeted even though they have done nothing extraordinary except stand as political opponents of a regime or another powerful social group. A new government may persecute people making speeches, handing out leaflets, and even attending a political meeting or rally. Or it may persecute members of a former regime's military. In many cases the persecution extends to officers' families or friends. To be granted asylum, applicants must prove their connection to this persecuted group.

The most difficult to pin down of the five grounds of persecution is "membership in a particular social group." This does not necessarily mean a formally organized group, but simply a class of people with a common characteristic. Cases that follow these criteria are less common but often receive attention in the media. They include women who claim persecution for being Westernized in an Islamic country; gay men or women who have been individually targeted by an oppressive government; or members of a disfavored professional association.

The United States has accepted African women asylees who fall under this category of persecution. Unlike many other asylees, these women did not flee a particular conflict, but an entire culture. In many African countries, including Mali, Sudan, Togo, and Egypt, all women and girls may undergo a procedure in which they are mutilated in the genital area. It is a horrifying, painful, and widespread practice.

The decision to accept refugees who feared genital mutilation presented a legal problem. The people conducting the procedure would argue that it is not meant specifically to punish or harm the women. As terrifying as it is, the traditionalists consider it to be a rite of passage into womanhood. Could this be persecution? A U.S. immigration court case in 1996 stated that it is. Fauziya Kassindja, a teenager from Togo who feared facing genital mutilation if she were forced to return to her home country, was granted asylum.

Asylum in the United States

Kassindja's asylum case is one example of the ongoing debates over what exactly defines persecution. While the Immigration and Nationality Act of 1965 does not define the term, U.S. courts and the Bureau of Citizenship and Immigration Services (BCIS)—formerly the Immigration and Naturalization Service (INS)—have reached a workable definition. Persecution as defined by the courts is "the infliction of suffering or harm on those who differ in a way that is regarded as offensive." Threats to life and freedom—including slavery, torture, and imprisonment without a trial—are always considered persecution. This includes genocide and state-sponsored murder as well. Threats of a lower magnitude, such as discrimination or harassment, are more open to consideration. The level of harm that would constitute persecution is decided by asylum officers and immigration courts. While individual cases

Since June 1996, the United States has accepted African women asylees who face the threat of female genitial mutilation (FGM) in their home country. In countries like Sudan, Mali, and Egypt, young African women are potential victims of this practice, which in some regions is considered a traditional rite of passage.

Refugee Resettlement

Refugees differ from asylees in that they are interviewed outside the United States before they are resettled. The interviews are done by immigration personnel, with policy guidance from the U.S. Department of State. Every year, in consultation with Congress, the president sets a ceiling on the number of refugees the United States will admit. In 2002 and 2003, President George W. Bush set a ceiling of 70,000 refugees. However, during these years new security procedures and bureaucratic problems resulted in the admission of far fewer refugees than this ceiling figure had anticipated.

There is no cap on the number of people who may be granted asylum in the United States in a given year. However, only 10,000 per year can become lawful permanent residents (allowed to stay permanently). Those who receive asylum but have not received one of these 10,000 slots are permitted to work; however, they do not enjoy other benefits of permanent residence, such as accruing time toward the five years required to be eligible for U.S. citizenship.

vary, officers and judges try to adhere to an established precedent in reaching a decision.

A surprisingly low number of people apply for asylum in the United States. From 1996 to 2000, fewer than 20,000 asylum applications a year were filed with INS asylum officers, though the number reached 25,000 in 2002. (This does not include cases filed directly before immigration judges during deportation proceedings.) The approval rates in cases filed with asylum officers have also been low—36 percent in 2002, 43 percent in 2001, and 20 percent from 1996 to 2000, according to official government statistics. In many cases, individuals won't even file for asylum if they or their attorneys think their cases are unlikely to be approved.

Individuals can apply for asylum in two ways. The first way is an affirmative application. This means that the asylum seeker has come forward of his or her own accord and asked the U.S. government for asylum. This may happen immediately upon arrival to the United States, but more often it happens after the individual has lived in the country for months. With an affirmative application, an asylum seeker will schedule an interview with an asylum officer to decide his or her case.

The second way to apply for asylum is a defensive application, which is conducted when an alien is in the middle of proceedings to be deported (formally removed from the country by U.S. authorities). Receiving asylum will prevent someone from being deported. The standard for getting asylum is the same here as with an affirmative application; however, since the applicant is already going through deportation proceedings, the claim is decided by an immigration judge instead of an asylum officer.

Waves of Asylees

It is common for asylum seekers to arrive to the United States in two waves. The first wave typically will consist of those with more resources and more schooling than those of later waves.

Asylum seekers with limited resources often must use improvised means of transport, as in the case of these Cubans who in 2003 braved the Florida Straits in a 1951 Chevrolet truck. Apprehended by the U.S. Coast Guard, the passengers of the makeshift boat were sent back to Cuba.

Some will already speak English, and most will have left their country for political reasons. Usually more individuals of the first wave are able to prove their claims than those arriving later.

Asylum seekers arriving later usually do not come as prepared. Because fewer of them speak English, they have a harder time adjusting to their new lives. They often receive assistance from the communities carved out by the earlier arrivals.

Asylees and refugees in the United States have attained some security, through both the self-sufficiency of their communities and the institution of permanent immigration laws; however, to a certain extent the status of these groups is affected by changes in public opinion. One of the primary factors affecting American attitudes toward asylum seekers is the state of the economy. When the economy is booming, refugees and asylees are welcomed, and people feel like they can afford to share the country's safety and prosperity and benefit from the contributions of newcomers. But when the economy stagnates and unemployment rises, some Americans start to see asylum seekers as a threat and fear that their jobs will be taken.

Another factor that has influenced American attitudes toward asylum seekers is terrorism, particularly in the months following the September 2001 terrorist attacks on New York and Washington, D.C. Despite high incidences of violent crime, particularly in urban centers, Americans have historically felt sheltered from the politically motivated violence taking place in the rest of the world. Any terrorism event of a high magnitude erases that feeling of security, and asylum seekers and other immigrants can subsequently be cast in a suspicious light.

Restrictionists and Humanitarians

Generally, public opinion shifts power between two impulses that guide asylum policy. There is the restrictionist camp, which wants to put stricter limits on all immigration. This camp views asylum seekers as a source of problems in the country, and therefore their entry into the country should be limited as much as possible.

The humanitarian camp has the opposite perspective and believes that the prosperity of the United States should be used to help people from other countries. While it is clear that assisting everyone is not really feasible, this camp favors a more open immigration policy, particularly in regard to victims of human rights abuses.

For a long period in U.S. history, there was a subgroup of this humanitarian camp with its own perspective on refugee policy. The anti-communists, active during the decades-long cold war between the United States and the Soviet Union, believed that American foreign policy should be dedicated to fighting communism wherever it spread. Anti-communists used refugee policy to further their agenda. By helping certain refugees and asylees, they argued, Americans were indirectly enfeebling a communist power while also helping its victims.

This thinking influenced asylum policy for decades but fizzled out with the end of the cold war. Today, the humanitarian camp seeks to direct its attention on the asylum seekers themselves, although there remains an underlying notion that providing assistance to refugees is an indirect way to combat the persecution committed by unjust governments.

2 IMMIGRATION AND ASYLUM POLICY

For over a century, the United States and Canada have used laws to control the flow of immigrants, including asylum seekers. But this was not always the case. North America was founded and built by immigrants, many of whom were escaping persecution much like the refugees of today.

In the 17th and 18th century, many groups who formed the colonies that would become the United States sought asylum, although it wasn't regulated like the present-day asylum system. The Puritans founded Massachusetts as a solution to escape religious persecution in England. Pennsylvania was a safe haven for the English Quakers, as well as German religious groups such as Moravians and Mennonites. Lord Baltimore, founder of Maryland, encouraged fellow Catholics to become colony members so that they could practice their religion without fear of persecution.

To better understand how asylum and asylees fit into the U.S. and Canadian immigration systems, it is helpful to take a look at the history of immigration in both countries.

A Short History of U.S. Immigration

Immigration to the United States has been characterized by openness punctuated by periods of restriction. During the 17th, 18th, and 19th centuries, immigration was essentially open without restriction, and, at times, immigrants were even recruited to come to America. Between 1783 and 1820,

◀ Immigrants wait to pass through customs at New York City's Ellis Island, 1905. Asylees join the millions of immigrants who move to North America for reasons other than to escape persecution.

approximately 250,000 immigrants arrived at U.S. shores. Between 1841 and 1860, more than 4 million immigrants came; most were from England, Ireland, and Germany.

Historically, race and ethnicity have played a role in legislation to restrict immigration. The Chinese Exclusion Act of 1882, which was not repealed until 1943, specifically prevented Chinese people from becoming U.S. citizens and did not allow Chinese laborers to immigrate for the next decade. An agreement with Japan in the early 1900s prevented most Japanese immigration to the United States.

Until the 1920s, no numerical restrictions on immigration existed in the United States, although health restrictions applied. The only other significant restrictions came in 1917, when passing a literacy test became a requirement for immigrants. Presidents Cleveland, Taft, and Wilson had vetoed similar measures earlier. In addition, in 1917 a prohibition was added to the law against the immigration of people from Asia (defined as the Asiatic barred zone). While a few of these prohibitions were lifted during World War II, they were not repealed until 1952, and even then Asians were only allowed in under very small annual quotas.

U.S. Immigration Policy from World War I to 1965

During World War I, the federal government required that all travelers to the United States obtain a visa at a U.S. consulate or diplomatic post abroad. As former State Department consular affairs officer C. D. Scully points out, by making that requirement permanent Congress, by 1924, established the framework of temporary, or non-immigrant visas (for study, work, or travel), and immigrant visas (for permanent residence). That framework remains in place today.

After World War I, cultural intolerance and bizarre racial theories led to new immigration restrictions. The House Judiciary Committee employed a eugenics consultant, Dr. Harry N. Laughlin, who asserted that certain races were inferior. Another leader of the eugenics movement, Madison Grant, argued that Jews, Italians, and others were inferior because of their supposedly different skull size.

The Immigration Act of 1924, preceded by the Temporary Quota Act of 1921, set new numerical limits on immigration based on "national origin." Taking effect in 1929, the 1924 act set annual quotas on immigrants that were specifically designed to keep out southern Europeans, such as Italians and Greeks. Generally no more than 100 people of the proscribed nationalities were permitted to immigrate.

While the new law was rigid, the U.S. Department of State's restrictive interpretation directed consular officers overseas to be even stricter in their application of the "public charge" provision. (A public charge is someone unable to support himself or his family.) As author Laura Fermi wrote, "In response to the new cry for restriction at the beginning of the [Great Depression] . . . the consuls were to interpret very strictly the clause prohibiting admission of aliens 'likely to become public charges; and to deny the visa to an applicant who in their opinion might become a public charge at any time.'"

In the early 1900s, more than one million immigrants a year came to the United States. In 1930—the first year of the national-origin quotas—approximately 241,700 immigrants were admitted. But under the State Department's strict interpretations, only 23,068 immigrants entered during 1933, the smallest total since 1831. Later these restrictions prevented many Jews in Germany and elsewhere in Europe from escaping what would become the Holocaust. At the height of the Holocaust in 1943, the United States admitted fewer than 6,000 refugees.

The Displaced Persons Act of 1948, the nation's first refugee law, allowed many refugees from World War II to settle in the United States. The law put into place policy changes that had already seen immigration rise from 38,119 in 1945 to 108,721 in 1946 (and later to 249,187 in 1950). One-third of those admitted between 1948 and 1951 were Poles, with ethnic

Germans forming the second-largest group.

The 1952 Immigration and Nationality Act is best known for its restrictions against those who supported communism or anarchy. However, the bill's other provisions were quite restrictive and were passed over the veto of President Truman. The 1952 act retained the national-origin quota system for the Eastern Hemisphere. The Western Hemisphere continued to operate without a quota and relied on other qualitative factors to limit immigration. Moreover, during that time, the Mexican bracero program, from 1942 to 1964, allowed millions of Mexican agricultural workers to work temporarily in the United States.

The 1952 act set aside half of each national quota to be divided among three preference categories for relatives of U.S. citizens and permanent residents. The other half went to aliens with high education or exceptional abilities. These quotas applied only to those from the Eastern Hemisphere.

A Halt to the National-Origin Quotas

The Immigration and Nationality Act of 1965 became a landmark in immigration legislation by specifically striking the racially based national-origin quotas. It removed the barriers to Asian immigration, which later led to opportunities to immigrate for many Filipinos, Chinese, Koreans, and others. The Western Hemisphere was designated a ceiling of 120,000 immigrants but without a preference system or per country limits. Modifications made in 1978 ultimately combined the Western and Eastern Hemispheres into one preference system and one ceiling of 290,000.

The 1965 act built on the existing system—without the national-origin quotas—and gave somewhat more priority to family relationships. It did not completely overturn the existing system but rather carried forward essentially intact the family immigration categories from the 1959 amendments to the Immigration and Nationality Act. Even though the text of the law prior to 1965 indicated that half of the immigration slots

President Lyndon Johnson signed the Immigration Act of 1965, inaugurating a new era of immigration. With the passage of the act, many foreign groups were able to immigrate to the United States in large numbers.

were reserved for skilled employment immigration, in practice, Immigration and Naturalization Service (INS) statistics show that 86 percent of the visas issued between 1952 and 1965 went for family immigration.

A number of significant pieces of legislation since 1980 have shaped the current U.S. immigration system. First, the Refugee Act of 1980 removed refugees from the annual world limit and established that the president would set the number of refugees who could be admitted each year after consultations with Congress.

Second, the 1986 Immigration Reform and Control Act (IRCA) introduced sanctions against employers who "knowingly" hired undocumented immigrants (those here illegally). It also provided amnesty for many undocumented immigrants.

Third, the Immigration Act of 1990 increased legal immigration by 40 percent. In particular, the act significantly increased the number of employment-based immigrants (to 140,000), while also boosting family immigration.

Fourth, the 1996 Illegal Immigration Reform and Immigrant Responsibility Act (IIRAIRA) significantly tightened rules that permitted undocumented immigrants to convert to legal status and made other changes that tightened immigration law in areas such as political asylum and deportation.

Fifth, in response to the September 11, 2001, terrorist attacks, the USA PATRIOT Act and the Enhanced Border Security and Visa Entry Reform Act tightened rules on the granting of visas to individuals from certain countries and enhanced the federal government's monitoring and detention authority over foreign nationals in the United States.

New U.S. Immigration Agencies

In a dramatic reorganization of the federal government, the Homeland Security Act of 2002 abolished the Immigration and Naturalization Service and transferred its immigration service

President Bush signs the Enhanced Border Security and Visa Entry Reform Act with congressional members in attendance, May 2002. The act, along with the USA PATRIOT Act, was passed in response to the September 2001 terrorist attacks.

and enforcement functions from the Department of Justice into a new Department of Homeland Security. The Customs Service, the Coast Guard, and parts of other agencies were also transferred into the new department.

The Department of Homeland Security, with regards to immigration, is organized as follows: The Bureau of Customs and Border Protection (BCBP) contains Customs and Immigration inspectors, who check the documents of travelers to the United States at air, sea, and land ports of entry; and Border Patrol agents, the uniformed agents who seek to prevent unlawful entry along the southern and northern border. The new Bureau of Immigration and Customs Enforcement (BICE) employs investigators, who attempt to find undocumented immigrants inside the United States, and Detention and Removal officers, who detain and seek to deport such individuals. The new Bureau of Citizenship and Immigration Services (BCIS) is where people go, or correspond with, to become U.S. citizens or obtain permission to work or extend their stay in the United States.

Following the terrorist attacks of September 11, 2001, the Department of Justice adopted several measures that did not require new legislation to be passed by Congress. Some of these measures created controversy and raised concerns about civil liberties. For example, FBI and INS agents detained for months more than 1,000 foreign nationals of Middle Eastern descent and refused to release the names of the individuals. It is alleged that the Department of Justice adopted tactics that discouraged the detainees from obtaining legal assistance. The Department of Justice also began requiring foreign nationals from primarily Muslim nations to be fingerprinted and questioned by immigration officers upon entry or if they have been living in the United States. Those involved in the September 11 attacks were not immigrants—people who become permanent residents with a right to stay in the United States—but holders of temporary visas, primarily visitor or tourist visas.

Immigration to the United States Today

Today, the annual rate of legal immigration is lower than that at earlier periods in U.S. history. For example, from 1901 to 1910 approximately 10.4 immigrants per 1,000 U.S. residents came to the United States. Today, the annual rate is about 3.5 immigrants per 1,000 U.S. residents. While the percentage of foreign-born people in the U.S. population has risen above 11 percent, it remains lower than the 13 percent or higher that prevailed in the country from 1860 to 1930. Still, as has been the case previously in U.S. history, some people argue that even legal immigration should be lowered. These people maintain that immigrants take jobs native-born Americans could fill and that U.S. population growth, which immigration contributes to, harms the environment. In 1996 Congress voted against efforts to reduce legal immigration.

Most immigrants (800,000 to one million annually) enter the United States legally. But over the years the undocumented (illegal) portion of the population has increased to about 2.8 percent of the U.S. population—approximately 8 million people in all.

Today, the legal immigration system in the United States contains many rules, permitting only individuals who fit into certain categories to immigrate—and in many cases only after waiting anywhere from 1 to 10 years or more, depending on the demand in that category. The system, representing a compromise among family, employment, and human rights concerns, has the following elements:

> U.S. citizen may sponsor for immigration a spouse, parent, sibling, or minor or adult child.
>
> A lawful permanent resident (green card holder) may sponsor only a spouse or child.
>
> A foreign national may immigrate if he or she gains an employer sponsor.
>
> An individual who can show that he or she has a "well-founded fear of persecution" may come to the country as a refugee—or be allowed to stay as an asylee (someone who receives asylum).

A bustling Chinatown market-place. The regular channels of immigration to the United States and Canada have fostered the establishment of Chinatowns and other ethnic enclaves in major cities.

Beyond these categories, essentially the only other way to immigrate is to apply for and receive one of the "diversity" visas, which are granted annually by lottery to those from "underrepresented" countries.

In 1996 changes to the law prohibited nearly all incoming immigrants from being eligible for federal public benefits, such as welfare, during their first five years in the country. Refugees were mostly excluded from these changes. In addition, families who sponsor relatives must sign an affidavit of support showing they can financially take care of an immigrant who falls on hard times.

A Short History of Canadian Immigration

In the 1800s, immigration into Canada was largely unrestricted. Farmers and artisans from England and Ireland made up a significant portion of 19th-century immigrants. England's Parliament passed laws that facilitated and encouraged the voyage to North America, particularly for the poor.

After the United States barred Chinese railroad workers from settling in the country, Canada encouraged the immigration of Chinese laborers to assist in the building of Canadian railways. Responding to the racial views of the time, the Canadian

Lester Pearson, prime minister of Canada from 1963 to 1968, believed that immigrants were key to the country's economic growth. In 1966 the Canadian government introduced a statement stressing the importance of an open immigration policy.

Parliament began charging a "head tax" for Chinese and South Asian (Indian) immigrants in 1885. The fee of $50—later raised to $500—was well beyond the means of laborers making one or two dollars a day. Later, the government sought additional ways to prohibit Asians from entering the country. For example, it decided to require a "continuous journey," meaning that immigrants to Canada had to travel from their country on a boat that made an uninterrupted passage. For immigrants or asylum seekers from Asia this was nearly impossible.

As the 20th century progressed, concerns about race led to further restrictions on immigration to Canada. These restrictions particularly hurt Jewish and other refugees seeking to flee persecution in Europe. Government statistics indicate that Canada accepted no more than 5,000 Jewish refugees before and during the Holocaust.

After World War II, Canada, like the United States, began accepting thousands of Europeans displaced by the war. Canada's laws were modified to accept these war refugees, as well as Hungarians fleeing Communist authorities after the crushing of the 1956 Hungarian Revolution.

The Immigration Act of 1952 in Canada allowed for a "tap on, tap off" approach to immigration, granting administrative authorities the power to allow more immigrants into the country in good economic times, and fewer in times of recession. The shortcoming of such an approach is that there is little evidence immigrants harm a national economy and much evidence they contribute to economic growth, particularly in the growth of the labor force.

In 1966 the government of Prime Minister Lester Pearson introduced a policy statement stressing how immigrants were key to Canada's economic growth. With Canada's relatively small population base, it became clear that in the absence of newcomers, the country would not be able to grow. The policy was introduced four years after Parliament enacted important legislation that eliminated Canada's own version of racially based national-origin quotas.

In 1967 a new law established a points system that awarded entry to potential immigrants using criteria based primarily on an individual's age, language ability, skills, education, family relationships, and job prospects. The total points needed for entry of an immigrant is set by the Minister of Citizenship and Immigration Canada. The new law also established a category for humanitarian (refugee) entry.

The 1976 Immigration Act refined and expanded the possibility for entry under the points system, particularly for those seeking to sponsor family members. The act also expanded refugee and asylum law to comport with Canada's international obligations. The law established five basic categories for immigration into Canada: 1) family; 2) humanitarian; 3) independents (including skilled workers), who immigrate to Canada on their own; 4) assisted relatives; and 5) business immigrants (including investors, entrepreneurs, and the self-employed).

The new Immigration and Refugee Protection Act, which took effect June 28, 2002, made a series of modifications to existing Canadian immigration law. The act, and the regulations that followed, toughened rules on those seeking asylum and the process for removing people unlawfully in Canada.

The law modified the points system, adding greater flexibility for skilled immigrants and temporary workers to become permanent residents, and evaluating skilled workers on the weight of their transferable skills as well as those of their specific occupation. The legislation also made it easier for employers to have a labor shortage declared in an industry or sector, which would facilitate the entry of foreign workers in that industry or sector.

On family immigration, the act permitted parents to sponsor dependent children up to the age of 22 (previously 19 was the maximum age at which a child could be sponsored for immigration). The act also allowed partners in common-law arrangements, including same-sex partners, to be considered as family members for the purpose of immigration sponsorship.

Along with these liberalizing measures, the act also included provisions to address perceived gaps in immigration-law enforcement.

Asylum Policy of the 20th Century

The atmosphere in the United States and Canada toward immigrants and asylum seekers before World War II was not welcoming. The period was marked by a depressed economy, restrictive laws, and negative stereotypes of foreigners, all of which contributed to a sense of inhospitality.

Perhaps the incident that most famously reflected this sentiment was the rejection of the refugees aboard an ocean liner known as the *St. Louis*. In May 1939, the *St. Louis* sailed from Hamburg, Germany. It carried 937 passengers, most of whom were emigrating Jews. They had filed for U.S. visas and

The ocean liner *St. Louis*, carrying 937 German Jewish refugees, was refused permission to dock in Miami in May 1939. It was forced to return its passengers to Europe, where they faced Nazi persecution.

planned to wait in Cuba for their authorization, but when the ship reached Havana, the passengers were rebuffed. Only a handful of the passengers who had proper paperwork could come ashore.

Looking for an alternative solution, the *St. Louis* tried to dock in Miami. The U.S. government refused to allow the ship into port, as did the Canadian government. Eventually, the *St. Louis* was forced to return to Europe, where the passengers resettled in Great Britain, the Netherlands, Belgium, and France. When Germany invaded Western European countries a few years later, a number of these Jewish refugees found their new homes over-run. Once again, they were subject to Nazi persecution. Many who could have been saved died in concentration camps.

After the war, changes to U.S. law finally made allowances for refugees. With the passing of the Displaced Persons Act of 1948, 205,000 refugees were permitted to enter the United States over the next two years. Groups that came in over quota would have slots taken out of the quotas for future years. The act was the first step toward legally recognizing asylum seekers.

United Nations High Commissioner for Refugees

The world's leading countries took the next step in 1950, establishing the United Nations High Commissioner for Refugees (UNHCR). UNHCR was put in place to find international solutions to refugee problems. In 1951, it directed its attention exclusively to the 400,000 refugees in Europe. Its budget was $300,000, and it had a staff of 33 people.

After more than 50 years in existence, UNCHR has grown dramatically. It now has over 100 offices, located all over the world. The $300,000 budget has increased to $1 billion, and its staff has grown to 5,000 people. Its mission has extended beyond helping refugees; now asylees, internally displaced people, returnees, and war-affected populations also receive assistance. Currently, UNHCR oversees 26 million people in crisis.

UNHCR's first action was adopting the 1951 Convention

Relating to the Status of Refugees. This treaty defined the term *refugee*. It also set down refugee rights, including that of non-refoulement. All those deemed refugees have the right to remain outside of their homeland. Countries who signed the Convention promised to honor those rights.

The United States did not sign the 1951 Convention, but it did sign the 1967 Protocol Relating to the Status of Refugees, which incorporates the terms of the Convention. Instead of following the course of action of most UN member countries, the United States developed its own way of dealing with refugees, which was informed greatly by cold war policy. Soon after the Second World War, relations between the U.S. and the Soviet Union cooled, due in large part to Soviet domination of Eastern European countries. The cold war pitted America's liberal democracy and capitalism against the Soviet Union's communism, but instead of putting armies on battlefields, the country's leaders fought ideological battles.

By the middle of the 1950s, the cold war agenda had worked its way into U.S. immigration policy. In 1955, the National Security Council of the Eisenhower administration issued a memorandum to fight international communism. The memo endorsed a variety of covert activities, including providing assistance to "refugee liberation groups." Any enemy of communism was thereafter deemed a friend of the United States.

Paroling Refugees

In October 1956, a popular revolt in Hungary temporarily ousted the communist regime. The Soviets responded by sending tanks and troops into the country to suppress the uprising. Tens of thousands of Hungarian refugees fled to Austria and Yugoslavia for safety.

Seeking to help the refugees, the U.S. attorney general used the authority to "parole" aliens into the United States. This procedure allowed people to enter the country but did not give them the right to stay permanently. Attorney General Herbert Brownell Jr. brought in 32,000 Hungarians this way, and

established a precedent for handling refugee crises that lasted until 1980.

Although Congress didn't control the flow of refugees, it could make decisions on their status once they arrived to the country. For example, in 1958 Hungarians were given the option to pursue permanent resident status. The next step for these lawful residents, if they wanted to take it, was to apply for citizenship.

Although the Immigration Act of 1965 opened up immigration to other ethnic groups, there were still a limited number of visas that were offered each year. Under the 1965 law, refugees would be accepted if they were fleeing communist countries, or

Soviet tanks station at strategic points of an intersection in Budapest, Hungary, to thwart the popular uprising of October 1956. In the wake of the Soviet invasion, the U.S. Attorney General authorized the entry of 32,000 Hungarians uprooted by the conflict.

fleeing from the Middle East and had a fear of persecution based on race, religion, or political opinion. Also, the law allowed the acceptance of refugees who were leaving a national or catastrophic disaster, although the disaster would have to be deemed severe enough by the president. Legislators believed that it was likely the clauses of the law could handle future refugee admissions, but the refugee crises during the second half of the 20th century would prove them wrong.

3 BOATLIFTS FROM THE CARIBBEAN

When the Eisenhower administration paroled the Hungarians fleeing the Soviet invasion in November 1956, a parole system for refugee admissions was set in motion. The system further meshed refugee admissions into the framework of U.S. foreign policy, and began a legacy that lasted decades and affected hundreds of thousands of lives.

During the 1950s, U.S. foreign policy was staunchly anti-communist. The refugee and asylum decisions made during that period—in particular the long-standing resolution to shelter Cuban exiles—reflect this stance.

In 1959, Fidel Castro overthrew Cuba's leader, General Fulgencio Batista. After cementing his power, Castro surrounded himself with hard-line communists. He nationalized U.S. businesses operating in Cuba, banned political parties, and shut down labor groups. Soon he controlled hospitals, newspapers, and radio stations. Step by step, Castro took control of everything. Those who opposed him were interrogated, imprisoned, or worse.

The First Exiles

Soon after Castro's revolution, Cubans began to leave the country. Members of Batista's government left the island first. Next to go were upper- and middle-class businessmen and their families. Many left for Spain or Latin America; others went to the United States, with which they generally were familiar.

◀ Cuban president Fidel Castro announces victory in the revolution to oust dictator Fulgencio Batista, January 1959. As a form of opposition to Castro's communist regime, instituted shortly after the revolution, the U.S. immigration system has provided asylum to Cuban exiles for over five decades.

Many had traveled to the United States before or had friends or contacts living there.

On the whole this first group of Cuban exiles was older and better educated than most immigrant groups, although because Castro ordered that no people bring any possessions out of the country, many arrived with hardly any money in 1961. They could carry no more than five dollars in their pockets.

Cuba kept the exiles' money, but it also lost a vast resource of talented people with plenty of initiative. Between January 1959 and April 1961, 125,000 Cubans arrived to the United States. Included in this group were the children of Operation Pedro Plan. Initiated by an American nonprofit organization in 1960, Operation Pedro Plan secured visas for orphaned Cuban children, and by 1962 had brought 14,000 children to the United States.

Although the United States planned to resettle Cuban exiles throughout the country, most settled in Miami, where there was a rapidly growing Cuban population. Eventually, Miami's "Little Havana" community also drew Cuban exiles living in Spain and Latin America.

For the refugees, the older individuals in particular, change was difficult. Because their manners were Cuban and they spoke a different language, many took jobs that required very little English. A number of the refugees were overqualified for their work—business managers became taxi drivers and short-order cooks. They hoped that they would live under these difficult circumstances for only a short period. Few people thought that the United States would allow a communist government to operate so close to its borders, and many believed Cuba would soon be liberated. Until that happened, the exiles planned to stay in Miami, where the climate was similar and the homeland was just a short plane flight away.

A Failed Invasion

In March 1960, the Central Intelligence Agency (CIA) began training an invading force of Cuban exiles, who would receive extensive support from the U.S. armed forces—or, at least that was the plan. Instead, shortly before the invasion, President Kennedy decided to pull the U.S. military out of the operation. The exiles landed unassisted at the Bay of Pigs in Cuba and met with strong resistance. Within three days, they were defeated.

The Cuban exiles' hopes for a quick return to their country had already begun to dwindle. The events of October 1962 nearly killed those hopes completely. During that month American spy planes detected missile silos in Cuba, where nuclear missiles had arrived from the Soviet Union. President Kennedy ordered the U.S. Navy to form a ring around Cuba, obstructing any ships from passing through. The world was on the brink of nuclear war, with Cuba at the center.

After 10 tense nights, the Soviets and the United States worked

President John F. Kennedy signs Proclamation 3504, authorizing a U.S. Navy quarantine of Cuba, in October 1962. The blockade was intended to keep Soviet ships carrying military supplies from reaching the island. The Cuban Missile Crisis was resolved when the Soviet Union agreed to remove its nuclear missiles from Cuba, and the United Sates agreed not to plan invasions of the island.

out a compromise. The Soviets promised not to bring missiles to Cuba, and the United States promised to stop funding Cuban freedom fighters and guerilla raids and to stop making invasion plans. All flights to the United States from Cuba were cancelled. Cuba remained under Castro's rule, and for three years very few people got in or out.

The situation changed abruptly in 1965. Discontent built up in Cuba to such a level that Castro decided he had to give potential defectors the opportunity to leave. Without warning, he announced that he was allowing Cubans to emigrate. Anyone who had family in the United States could get a visa to leave Cuba, and he invited Cubans living in the United States to pick up their family members at Camarioca harbor. Thousands of small boats made the trip. Over 5,000 migrants arrived in the United States before the INS stopped the boatlift.

The sudden departure of so many migrants resulted in chaos. Cubans demanded a more organized emigration procedure, and as a result, direct plane flights from Cuba were resumed. People would regularly fly from Havana to the United States on what were called "freedom flights." The new plan would be legal and orderly, unlike previous boatlifts, or those that would take place later.

In the 1960s and 1970s, the attorney general's authority to parole people into the United States gave Cubans the permission to stay lawfully in the country. However, their status as permanent residents (green card holders) was not guaranteed. The Cuban Adjustment Act, passed in 1966, was a crucial piece of legislation that addressed this issue, and over the decades it has guided much of U.S. policy towards Cuban refugees. The law allows Cubans to become green card holders after being physically present in the United States for one year or more, regardless of how they first arrived to the country. Between 1946 and 1998, approximately 618,000 Cubans adjusted to permanent residence, according to the Congressional Research Service.

Cuba and the 1980 Refugee Act

During the decades that large waves of Cuban refugees arrived and were resettled, the United States was gradually expanding on its definition of a refugee. The United Nations had encouraged world leaders to broaden their perspective on the issue. The 1967 Protocol Relating to the Status of Refugees made slight changes to the refugee definition, removing it from the specific context of World War II and expanding its application beyond Europe to the rest of the world.

As presidential administrations changed, so did asylum policy. In 1979 President Jimmy Carter formed the office of the U.S. Coordinator for Refugee Affairs, and the following year in March he signed the Refugee Act of 1980. Thereafter, the way in which the United States handled refugees and asylees was fundamentally different.

First, the act redefined the term *refugee*. Before it was passed, there was one important difference between the American definition and the UN definition. The older American definition specified that refugees were fleeing communist countries, but the Refugee Act removed that anti-communist language.

The act also enabled the setting of an annual refugee ceiling, which was viewed as a more efficient mechanism than parole. The first ceiling was set at 50,000 refugees for the next two years, and higher ceilings were set in following years. The law also made refugees eligible for certain social programs and allowed them to apply for permanent resident status after living one year in the country.

Yet another change instituted by the Refugee Act had immediate consequences. Asylum was now recognized as separate from the refugee system. The act stated the attorney general must develop an asylum procedure for aliens, regardless of their status. Anyone in the United States who met the requirements could request asylum and stay if he or she met the legal definition. It was now possible to find safety in the United States, no matter how someone made it into the country.

The Boatlifts of 1980

The new asylum legislation had immediate consequences for Cuban exiles. In April 1980, three weeks later after the Refugee Act was passed, Fidel Castro opened Mariel harbor, letting Cubans leave if they wished. Thousands of Cubans soon crowded into small boats. The Straits of Florida teemed with barely seaworthy vessels. At its height of what became known as the Mariel boatlift, the Coast Guard picked up 5,000 Cubans each day. Nearly 125,000 Cubans applied for asylum after reaching the United States.

By June, the numbers of Cubans who were reaching South Florida every day were overwhelming. Accessing the magnitude of the situation, President Carter decided to put the new asylum privileges on hold and instead assign the recently arrived Cubans a special entrant status. They were not granted auto-

A boat full of Cuban refugees arrives in Key West, Florida, as part of the massive Mariel boatlift of 1980, which entailed the sudden influx of more than 125,000 refugees. After the Refugee Act of 1980 was passed, these refugees were protected from deportation.

matic asylum, but they were protected from deportation until their status was resolved. The procedure was the equivalent of parole, even though the new law officially ended that process.

Despite Carter's decision to suspend certain asylum privileges, a large percentage of the Cubans fleeing in 1980 were eventually granted asylum. In contrast, the Haitians fleeing persecution at the time—estimated to number more than 5,000—were treated quite differently. Many didn't make it to the United States at all.

U.S. Asylum Policy and Haiti

After Cuba turned communist in 1959, the U.S. government had adopted a strategy of preventing Haiti from becoming a communist state. The first move was to make sure that Haiti's dictator, François Duvalier, stayed in power. Duvalier ruled the country from 1957 to 1971. During those years, Haiti maintained its pro-Western policies, but its people were beset with widespread poverty and government corruption. They had no genuine political freedom. Political leaders, activists, and journalists faced the danger of being arrested and interrogated at any time.

Despite the problems facing Haiti, the U.S. and Haitian governments were continually building stronger ties. Because these relations were always improving, the United States could not justify granting Haitian migrants automatic asylum. Taking in refugees from a non-communist ally did not fit in with the current agenda.

However, Haiti would continue to neglect the democratic process, which made the U.S. policy regarding Haitian refugees more controversial. When François Duvalier died in 1971, and his son Jean-Claude took over, the country turned for the worse. Arrests became more frequent, and interrogations became crueler. By 1972, a Haitian exodus was in motion. Over the next eight years, approximately 30,000 Haitians entered the United States by boat. Thousands of them sought asylum, but fewer than 100 were approved.

President François "Papa Doc" Duvalier (1907–71) ushered in an era of government repression in Haiti that continued with his son, Jean-Claude ("Baby Doc"), the country's president from 1971 to 1986. Although many Haitians were victims of persecution during the Duvalier era, the United States only granted asylum to a limited number of Haitians.

Unlike Cubans, Haitians picked up at sea by the Coast Guard were considered "excludable." Until 1974, they were returned to Haiti without a hearing. In 1975, an American organization known as the National Council of Churches (NCC) sued the INS, claiming that it had treated Haitian refugees unfairly and was following a double standard. The NCC invoked the 1967 Protocol, which had become the bill of rights for refugees, and argued that by returning Haitians to Haiti, the United States was violating refugees' rights. The churches' case was denied, but other cases were filed in its wake.

Organizations advocating for the Haitians were encouraged by the passing of the 1980 Refugee Act, which broke down the last remaining legal justification for using a double standard against Cubans and Haitians. With the anti-communist language removed from the refugee definition, Haitian applicants could now at least be considered for the same status that individuals from communist countries received. In July 1980, a federal district judge acknowledged that a double standard was being used, and he halted the deportation of more than 4,000 Haitians. He ruled that their cases were not heard with the same care as

Cubans. He also accused the INS of acting on a bias, and ordered that the courts hear another round of individual cases.

Like Cubans, Haitians at this stage were now protected from deportation until they received a fair hearing. Haitian and Cuban hearings would continue to take place, and in accordance with the policy, both groups would receive equal treatment.

A New Policy of Interdiction

After President Ronald Reagan took office in 1981, his administration sought to stop the asylum cases at their source. He issued an executive order to the Coast Guard to intercept Haitian boats and tow them back to Port-au-Prince, Haiti. This procedure was called interdiction. Those Haitians who made it past the Coast Guard were now placed in guarded camps. They were held without bail, and were almost always deported afterward. From a restrictionist standpoint, Reagan's policy was effective. Very few Haitians made it to the United States in 1981; the year before, 12,000 Haitians had arrived.

The Reagan administration's interdiction policy was by no means popular with everyone. Amnesty International, a human rights organization, testified that Haitian refugees were in real danger if they returned to Haiti. The United Nations High Commissioner for Refugees opposed interdiction as well, arguing that Haitians were not being given a fair hearing. The Coast Guard's response to these accusations was that it was conducting hearings at sea. With or without hearings, however, the results were still the same: according to the Congressional Research Service, 22,940 Haitians were intercepted at sea between 1981 and 1990, with only 11 allowed to apply for asylum by the U.S. government.

Some who opposed the administration's policy claimed that interdiction was no less severe than Thailand's refusal of thousands of Vietnamese refugees during that time. After the Vietnam War, South Vietnamese refugees took to the sea to escape the recently installed communist government. The "boat

people," as they were called, were kept from ports of the region. In Thailand, they were pushed away by the country's army at gunpoint. Many Vietnamese died at sea from starvation, exposure, and drowning.

Despite the similarities observed by human rights groups between the American policy of interdiction and the Thai army's refusal of the refugees, there were significant differences. The U.S. Coast Guard was safely towing boats back to port, not pushing them out to sea. Also, the Reagan administration interpreted the 1967 Protocol to apply only to areas within U.S. borders. Because interdiction took place on international waters, it was technically not refoulement. Although UNHCR and other organizations contested this defense, the Supreme Court ultimately supported the Reagan administration's stance.

Haiti's situation temporarily improved with the election of its first president, Jean-Bertrand Aristide, in 1991. President George H. W. Bush ended the interdictions, but then they were resumed after a military coup in September of that year led to a new exodus from Haiti.

By spring of 1992 the Coast Guard had intercepted 38,000

Haitian refugees are interdicted at sea and brought aboard a U.S. Coast Guard ship in 1991. After a brief seven-month period of stability during that year, which began with the democratic election of President Jean-Bertrand Aristide, a coup in September spurred another wave of refugees to leave the country.

Haitians since Aristide was forced from power. Many were brought to the U.S. naval base at Guantánamo Bay and more than 10,400 were paroled into the United States after they were screened and found to have a credible fear of persecution. The parole gave them at least an opportunity to gain asylum through a complete interview with the INS.

However, in May 1992 President Bush ordered the Coast Guard to intercept all Haitians in boats and immediately return them without interviews. This was a controversial decision that human rights organizations considered a violation of international law. In July the 2nd Circuit Court of Appeals ruled against the Bush administration's policy of denying individual Haitians a screening for refugee status. However, the Supreme Court did not uphold the ruling.

Asylum Corps and Temporary Protected Status

The asylum system was further modified during the administration of George H. W. Bush. In 1990, final regulations were added to the Refugee Act of 1980 that separated asylum procedures from other INS matters. Legislators had acted in the hope that the asylum process would be less influenced by political agendas. The INS established an "Asylum Corps" of specially trained officers who would exclusively work on asylum cases. These officers began keeping files on countries of origin, making it easier to gather information on applicants' backgrounds.

The new regulations also set a limit of only 90 days to process an asylum request. If an applicant did not have an interview by then, he or she would be granted a work permit until the case was decided. However, a combination of factors led to a staggering backlog of asylum cases. The understaffed Asylum Corps labored to keep pace, and the process was further complicated by false asylum claims to get work permits.

Finally, this legislation brought into existence "Temporary Protected Status." As long as asylum seekers have this status, they can find work and stay in the United States without fear of deportation. It is granted to a person of a particular nationality for a period of 6 to 18 months, and can be renewed if conditions in a homeland country still warrant it, such as an ongoing war or the effects of a natural disaster.

Refugee Interviews at Sea

In 1994, the United States began testing a new way to handle refugees from Haiti, which was still in a state of upheaval following the overthrow of President Aristide in 1991. The U.S. government set up a refugee application center on board the hospital ship the USNS *Comfort*. Many asylum claims were processed in this manner. However, soon there was an overload of applicants, and the United States decided to put a halt to processing aboard the ship. New migrants were instead held in a base at Guantánamo Bay. If they were found to be in

U.S. Coast Guardsmen handle a Haitian baby after a boat of migrants is interdicted off the coast of Haiti. During the 1990s and the opening years of the 21st century, U.S. presidents maintained a policy of interdiction with Haitians, in most cases turning migrants back to their country if they are stopped at sea.

danger, they could stay in the base's cramped but safe camp; otherwise, they would be taken back to Haiti. That October, the United States helped restore President Aristide to power, and most people returned to Haiti soon afterward.

Around this time, there was a new wave of Cuban immigrants, which in part arose from the fall of the Soviet Union and subsequent downturn of the Cuban economy. President Bill Clinton responded by expanding interdiction to include Cuban refugees, a practice that continues to this day. In September 1994 the United States and Cuba reached a compromise on the refugee issue. The United States agreed it would take Cubans interdicted at sea to a "safe haven" outside U.S. territory rather than processing them on the mainland as they had done before. The U.S. government also agreed to admit into the United States—through legal channels—a minimum of 20,000 Cuban immigrants a year in addition to the immediate relatives of Cubans who had become U.S. citizens.

In the years following this agreement, the U.S. Coast Guard continued its efforts to keep Cuban rafters out. This plan has involved such extremes as wrestling with Cubans in the surf before they reach land. However, once Cubans make it to American soil, they are still virtually guaranteed asylum.

Asylum policy regarding Haitians remained controversial during the administration of George W. Bush, who took office in 2001. At the end of that year, the U.S. government started to detain almost all Haitians who made it to U.S. soil via boat. Attorney General John Ashcroft argued that the policy was necessary to prevent a "mass migration" and, in the spring 2003, invoked "national security" to justify the continuing detention of the Haitians.

4 CENTRAL AMERICA

Throughout the 1980s, war and political persecution drove more than 2 million people from their homes. Nicaragua, El Salvador, and Guatemala were engulfed in internal conflicts. Many people fled to neighboring countries, and from there some entered the United States illegally. Of the people who crossed the U.S. border, some promptly requested asylum; others waited until they were more ready. Still others claimed it only as a defense against deportation.

Nicaragua

President Anastasio Somoza ruled Nicaragua from 1937 to 1947, and then again from 1950 to 1956. Facing a similar situation as that involving the Duvaliers in Haiti, the United States supported Somoza in the hopes of thwarting the spread of communism in the Western Hemisphere. In 1979 a Marxist group known as the Sandinistas disrupted the U.S. plan by overthrowing the Nicaraguan government. The Sandinistas drove Somoza and his military leaders out of the country. Civilians with ties to the exile government soon followed in the military leaders' path.

On the whole, the anti-communist Nicaraguans were welcomed into the United States and their asylum claims were accepted. The 20,000 undocumented Nicaraguans whose asylum claims were not yet decided—but who still deserved closer

◀ Former Guatemalan dictator Efraín Rios Montt signs an official registration to become a presidential candidate in the election of November 2003. Because Montt was accused of committing genocide during his regime in the early 1980s, which produced thousands of Guatemalan asylum seekers, the country's courts disputed his candidacy.

consideration—were granted a status that would temporarily save them from being deported.

Instead of going to the United States, many Nicaraguans fled to neighboring Honduras. There a guerilla group called the Contras formed and devised plans to retake Nicaragua from the Sandinistas. The Reagan administration supported this endeavor and funneled nearly $20 million in weapons to the contras. Some Cuban exiles left the United States to help the Contras, including Cuban American doctors who provided medical assistance.

Guatemala and El Salvador

Guatemala was in political turmoil throughout the 1980s. The country passed through a series of revolts that ended with the installation of General Efraín Rios Montt's bloody regime. Leftist guerillas challenged Montt's rule, and Montt responded by drafting an army of civilian defense patrols, which routed the guerillas in several fierce battles.

Over 200,000 civilians were killed in the fighting, and nearly one million people lost their homes. Meanwhile, the Guatemalan military tortured and executed people as part of an attempt to hold power. The guerillas used similar tactics, leaving much of the innocent civilian population caught in the middle. During Montt's rule, tens of thousands of civilians were killed or disappeared. Thousands of people fled the war zone. The United States accepted relatively few as political refugees, considering most to be "economic migrants" and not eligible for asylum.

El Salvador, which is situated between Guatemala and Nicaragua, suffered through its own civil war. The Nicaraguan Sandinista government armed five guerilla groups that challenged the Salvadoran government. The Reagan administration responded, granting El Salvador nearly $4 billion in military aid. Once again, civilians became victims in the fray, and approximately 70,000 were killed. Many of those who survived left El Salvador for safer ground. Over the next two

Nicaraguan president Anastasio Somoza (1925–80) led the country for two separate terms in the 1960s and 1970s. He received U.S. support against the Marxist Sandistinas, but the U.S. government eventually dropped its allegiance, and in 1979 he was deposed and assassinated. Some anti-communist Nicaraguans in the United States were granted asylum, and many were at least protected from deportation.

years, nearly a half-million Salvadorans entered the United States illegally.

U.S. border patrols reported many Salvadoran migrants. The White House maintained they were fleeing the communist rebels rather than the governments that the U.S. government supported. For this reason, the asylum claims of most Salvadorans migrants during that period were rejected. In 1983, only 2 percent of 13,000 Salvadoran applicants were granted asylum.

The Refugee Act of 1980 made it easier for migrants from non-communist countries in Central America to be granted asylum. However, many believed that the U.S. foreign policy of the State Department swayed the asylum decisions of the INS.

UNHCR opposed the United States' treatment of Salvadoran migrants, but could not convince the government to change its policy. Concerned church associations and human rights groups also protested, but to no avail.

The Sanctuary Movement and the ABC Case

After lobbying did not produce any successful results, some church groups decided to take the issues facing Salvadoran and Guatemalan migrants into their own hands. The groups, collectively known as the Sanctuary movement, began helping the migrants illegally enter the United States. The volunteers described their work as an exercise in civil disobedience, which means they broke laws they considered unjust in order to serve a greater good. Churches hid migrants in church basements, monasteries, and people's homes. They smuggled some people into Canada, where the asylum system was less driven by foreign policy. Sanctuary volunteers, including cofounder Reverend John Fife, were tried and convicted of criminal misconduct. The movement saved some lives, and the publicity that accompanied the trials attracted attention to the migrant crisis. Still, government policy concerning the Central Americans did not change.

Other church groups directly fought the asylum policy in court. In 1990 the Department of Justice finally settled the case of *American Baptist Churches of the U.S.A. v. Meese*, also known as "the *ABC* Case." The court decision ordered that over 150,000 Salvadorans and Guatemalans could apply for asylum under new rules. The decision affected people who had already been denied asylum—even those who were served with deportation papers. These people could now reapply for asylum.

During the early 1990s, the migrants' advocates observed that the asylum hearings were not being as conducted as fairly as they should and pushed for legislation to address the issue. In 1997, after much wrangling in Congress, President Bill

Clinton signed the Nicaraguan Adjustment and Central American Relief Act (NACARA). This law made it easier for the more than 150,000 Guatemalan and Salvadoran migrants who were part of the *ABC* class action suit to stay in the United States and eventually apply for permanent resident status. It also gave some tens of thousands of Nicaraguans and Cubans who had arrived in the United States before 1995 the right to lawful permanent residence.

5 THE ASYLUM LAW CHANGES OF 1996

Just days after the inauguration of President Bill Clinton in 1993, a man named Mir Aimal Kansi fired on employees of the CIA outside its headquarters in Langley, Virginia. Bullets hit five people and claimed two lives.

Kansi was a native of Pakistan who had applied for asylum in 1992. By the time of the shooting he had still not gone through an asylum interview to decide his case. The tragedy pointed out the flaws in the asylum system. Asylum officers had been too overwhelmed with other cases to give proper, speedy attention to Kansi's application.

Doubts about the effectiveness of the asylum system were raised again a month later when another asylum applicant was involved in a violent attack. In 1992 Rasmzi Ahmed Yousef, an Iraqi, had been detained at an airport where he claimed asylum. After making his application, Yousef was allowed to leave. On February 26, 1993, he drove a Ryder truck filled with explosives into the parking garage of the World Trade Center in New York City. Over 1,000 people were injured by the explosion, and 6 people died.

Following these incidents, people began to perceive asylum less as providing refuge for people in danger and more as a legal loophole. Sadly, this perception was not entirely unjustified. The system was overloaded. In May 1992, there were 244,000 pending cases, and almost 425,000 cases in the

◀ Emergency workers assist a woman injured in the World Trade Center bombing in February 1993, which killed six people and injured over 1,000 others. Following the bombing, the U.S. asylum system faced criticism after it was revealed that foreign nationals involved in the attack might have been deported, were it not for a massive case backlog that left their asylum claims pending for several months.

A woman receives oxygen after the 1993 World Trade Center bombing. Changes to U.S. immigration law occurred in the years after the 1993 attack, and again after the attacks on the Pentagon and the World Trade Center in 2001.

backlog by 1994. People who filed for asylum would sometimes wait years for an interview. While they waited, they were issued temporary papers allowing them to work in the United States until their cases were resolved. In some cases, issuing these papers allowed those without legitimate claims to exploit the system.

A month after the 1993 World Trade Center bombing, the asylum system's image was dealt yet another blow. New York's INS director William Slattery appeared on the newsmagazine *60 Minutes* to speak about the backlog of cases. The news story drew a correlation between the holes in the asylum system with the recent terrorist attacks, and it portrayed asylum as an easy way to avoid deportation and get working papers. Many human rights advocates believed this broadcast helped shape later criticisms of the U.S. asylum system.

Asylum Reform

One of the advocates for more restrictive asylum laws was Florida Congressman Bill McCollum, who introduced a bill calling for the summary exclusion of asylum seekers. (In the Senate, fellow Republican Alan Simpson of Wyoming introduced a bill with similar measures.) A proposed solution to the asylum backlog, the summary exclusion provision authorized immigration inspectors at airports and other ports of entry to decide on the spot whether asylum seekers had a legitimate fear of persecution. If asylum seekers were found to have legitimate claims, they would enter the asylum system but usually after a

Republican Representative Bill McCollum called for tougher asylum laws during the mid-1990s, when he introduced what was known as the "summary exclusion" bill. Portions of his bill, in modified form, became law in 1996.

period of detention. If their claims were rejected, they would be sent back to their home country on the next plane. (*A Well-Founded Fear: The Congressional Battle to Save Political Asylum in America*, written by Georgetown University Law School Professor Philip Schrag, is the best book on the changes to political asylum in the 1990s and the source of much of the information provided here.)

Summary exclusion had been brought before Congress and the Senate before. During the Reagan administration, when the asylum backlog had just begun to grow, Senator Simpson had proposed similar changes to the asylum system as part of a broader immigration bill. Simpson also had proposed a 35-day deadline to apply for asylum. He asserted that if someone comes to the United States for protection, that person should know the reason and be able to declare it within a month.

Attorneys and human rights advocates argued that the Simpson clauses were unfair. According to the opponents, the clauses failed to acknowledge the situation facing asylum seekers who may have recently experienced a trauma, or the difficulties they may have following U.S. legal procedures and securing an attorney for an asylum case. Also, in many situations individuals delay their application for a few months because they are waiting to see if conditions in their home country will improve enough that they can return. Finally, Simpson's opponents argued, a premature application can sometimes cost asylum seekers later on in their own country, particularly in places where people who apply for asylum in the United States are castigated by their political enemies.

Republican Senator Alan Simpson fought for immigration restrictions in the 1980s and 1990s. In 1996, asylum restrictions proposed by Simpson and others were written into law with the passing of the Illegal Immigration Reform and Immigrant Responsibility Act (IIRIRA).

Simpson's proposals were ultimately considered too drastic by the Democrat-controlled Senate. When the Immigration Reform and Control Act was passed in 1986, it did not include any changes to asylum law (although parts of the law affected asylees as much as other immigrants). But in 1995, Simpson judged the time was right to reintroduce his provisions, with the asylee cause much less popular than it was in the early 1980s. Also, Republicans now constituted a majority in Congress.

Cutting Down the Case Backlog

The Clinton administration hired immigration expert David Martin as a consultant to reform the asylum system. Martin was a law professor and under the Carter administration had worked on Haitian asylum cases for the State Department's human rights office. In 1995 Martin developed a number of procedural reforms to eliminate the backlog and to allow the asylum system to run more smoothly.

The new regulations gave asylum officers 180 days to complete a case before work papers were issued. This doubled the amount of time the system had to process claims (often cases are scheduled within 60 days). In addition, asylum applicants were not given automatic work authorization while their application was pending, thus removing the incentive to file asylum solely to gain legal work status. Finally, the most recently filed applications would be handled first, and the backlog would be dealt with as time permitted. This made it much less likely that an applicant would get working papers simply because officers failed to meet the deadline.

The new changes made a big difference. After they took effect in January 1995, new asylum applications dropped 44 percent. Ironically, once much of the fraud had been removed from the system, the asylum approval rate increased.

A New Republican Majority

Despite the success of the reforms, from a political standpoint they had arrived too late. The 1994 congressional election gave much control of the two houses to the Republican Party. Control of the houses is pivotal, not just because it gives a party an advantage in the vote, but also because it determines the leadership of committees and subcommittees. This leadership subsequently helps decide the type of bill that receives a vote in Congress—or if the bill reaches the floor at all. The Republican majority that existed after the 1994 election was a primary factor behind the passing of the historic 1996 Illegal Immigration Reform and Immigrant Responsibility Act (IIRIRA).

Immigration subcommittees are overseen by judiciary committees, which consider each bill before it reaches the floor of the full House or Senate. After the Republicans regained control of Congress, Representative Lamar Smith became chair of the House Immigration Subcommittee. Smith aggressively sought an immigration reform bill, and in the Senate Alan Simpson followed a similar agenda.

On January 24, 1995, Simpson introduced the first immigration bill, which dealt with a number of issues covering both legal and undocumented immigrants. It included a cap on the number of refugees allowed into the United States each year, as well as provisions for summary exclusion. It also brought another old proposal of Simpson's back to the table—a deadline for asylum seekers. Philip Schrag notes how these measures were problematic for legitimate asylum seekers. The most restrictive measure was the 30-day deadline for asylum applications, which threatened to prevent many deserving applicants from receiving asylum.

Most asylum applicants require a period of more than 30 days to apply for asylum. There are a few reasons for these application delays: One, asylum seekers may not yet know what asylum is, or how to get it; some may expect that they receive it automatically upon reaching U.S. shores. Two, the asylum system is intimidating, especially to the people who need it the most. To get help filling out the application form, many asylees seek a lawyer or representative, which takes time, especially if they don't speak English. Thirty days can seem like a long time, but in a foreign country with an unfamiliar language and set of customs, it's often not a long enough period to find the right legal assistance.

The House Bill

Lamar Smith, who coordinated with Senator Simpson on the asylum reforms, introduced a bill similar to Simpson's in the House. After a bill like this is introduced, it goes into the markup process in its committee. During markup, committee members debate changes to a bill that are voted on by the entire committee.

Lobbyists also try to convince legislators to vote a certain way during this stage. The House and Senate immigration bills sparked the creation of a new lobby group—the Committee to Protect Asylum (CPA), made up primarily of human rights and legal organizations. A founding member of the committee, Philip Schrag documents its goals and methods in *A Well-Founded Fear*. Members of the CPA wrote letters to newspapers, called congressional offices, and brought asylees to face-to-face meetings with legislators. Their main goal was to eliminate the asylum deadline and modify other provisions.

The Senate Bill

During the markup stage of the asylum bill debate, the Senate bill had been modified more than the House bill. The asylum deadline in the Senate bill was extended from 30 days to 1 year. Also, it applied only to people making defensive asylum claims against being deported, and exceptions to the deadline could be made if asylum seekers showed "good cause." These exceptions included physical or mental disabilities, fear for one's family abroad, changed circumstances in the applicant's country of origin, or the unavailability of professional assistance. The INS was also allowed to add more exceptions as it saw fit.

In addition, the Senate bill repealed the summary exclusion procedures that had been included in a recently passed anti-terrorism bill. Earlier in the year, the House had drafted and passed an anti-terrorism bill that included broad summary exclusion powers. Although it was presented as a terrorism bill, the summary exclusion provision had not been limited to terrorists and people suspected of terrorism, but applied to anyone who entered the United States without the proper documents. The immigration bill that reached the House floor was more restrictive, letting the summary exclusion provisions stand. Also, the asylum deadline was only modified to six months, and applied to people making both affirmative and defensive claims.

Finding a Compromise

The next stage in the legislative process was to reconcile these two bills. This is done in a conference committee, which includes members of both houses. Often members of both parties work out a compromise, ironing out the differences between the two bills. In the case of the immigration bill, something different happened. In his account of the events, Schrag contends that the Republicans from the House and the Senate met in private, making agreements in a series of pre-conference meetings. When the full conference committee met at last, most differences had been worked out with no input from the Democratic legislators.

The conference itself was largely a formality. The bill had already been written, and the conference committee's chairman, Lamar Smith, allowed no Democratic amendments to be heard. The bill that emerged was severe in a number of areas, using the more restrictive House bill as the main text. Some other changes were made. The term "summary exclusion" changed to "expedited removal," though with only one major differ-ence, the provision basically retained the same function. Expedited removal would apply to anyone stopped at a port of entry without a visa or passport, but not to others. The one difference was that people who contested their expedited removal would have the right to appeal, although they were allowed a week to prepare their case. The asylum deadline was extended to one full year, but the Senate's detailed definition of having "good cause" to file late was struck from the bill.

The Battle over Asylum Ends

On September 25, 1996, the House of Representatives passed the Illegal Immigration Reform and Immigrant Responsibility Act with a vote of 305 to 123. Five days later, President Clinton signed the bill into law.

When the president signs a bill, it often seems like the end of the story. In reality, this is just the beginning in many ways. After the law is signed, it must be put into practice. There are many steps between the broad language of a law and the act of enforcing it. In other words, once a law is written everyone must comply; however, many laws leave some room for interpretation.

Philip Schrag describes how at the enforcement level, asylum advocates tempered some of the harsher provisions of the 1996 act. The INS was convinced to apply broader interpretations to the two exceptions to the one-year deadline, which fell under the designations "changed circumstances" and "extraordinary circumstances." The regulations set out specific conditions under which these exceptions would apply and gave asylum officers discretion within the framework of the regulations.

Also, the regulations stated that expedited removal would only be used on people who were stopped at ports of entry without the right documents. It would not be used for people who did not use ports of entry (such as the many Mexican border crossings) or for those who were approved to enter the country but were later deemed deportable.

The immigration laws of the 1990s introduced stringent measures, but those measures were eased somewhat in their execution. In effect, the long battle over political asylum ended in a draw.

6 THE ASYLUM PROCESS, STEP BY STEP

Unlike refugees, asylum applicants get to the United States on their own power. They only apply for asylum once they have arrived. U.S. law allows any number of people to be granted asylum in a year; however, under the law, only up to 10,000 people each year may become lawful permanent residents.

Asylees arrive in a number of ways. Some arrive illegally, desperate to escape the dangerous conditions of their homeland. Others arrive legally on temporary visas, and decide to apply for asylum only after learning their country has recently become a dangerous place to live.

Some immigrant groups, like those from Cuba, Dominican Republic, and Haiti, are close enough to sail to the United States. They may use their own boats or travel with a neighbor or family, or they may contact professional smugglers, who charge a high price for transport.

Some people stow away on airplanes. Flying in this manner is particularly dangerous, with the cold temperatures at high altitudes dropping to 60 degrees below zero. In 1997, two Indian men stowed away in an airplane's wheel compartment. One man survived the 10-hour flight, but his younger brother froze to death and fell from the plane. In December 2002, a man also successfully flew from Cuba to Canada in a wheel well. The week before, two boys from the African country of

◀ A U.S. Navy ship transports Cuban refugees who were picked up at sea while trying to reach the United States. In recent decades, hundreds of thousands of migrants from Caribbean countries like Cuba, the Dominican Republic, and Haiti have attempted to reach the United States in ships, boats, and even rafts.

Ghana tried the same method of escape, but both died from the lack of oxygen and freezing temperatures.

Leaving a hostile country can be as challenging a problem as arriving in a safe one. Families often offer aid in the escape. People will bribe guards to set imprisoned family members free. Additional money and connections will go a long way toward finally getting someone out of the country. Assistance can come from strangers as well as friends and family—supporters of the Sanctuary movement of the 1980s volunteered to smuggle Guatemalans and Salvadorans into the United States. It is also common for sympathetic groups to provide false passports and money for a plane ticket.

Arriving to a Port of Entry

Asylum seekers may discover that the ordeal has not ended upon arriving to North America. Because of the expedited removal provisions of the 1996 Illegal Immigration Reform and Immigrant Responsibility Act, anyone stopped at a U.S. port of entry without a valid passport or visa can be refused entry. Unless asylum seekers claim a fear of persecution in their home country, they can be deported without a hearing. Some may not realize what is happening until they have missed their chance. However, in keeping with the U.S. government's airport procedures, an asylum officer is obligated to conduct an initial interview with an applicant. This is called a "credible fear" interview, since it determines if the applicant has reason to fear returning home. Applicants found with a legitimate claim are forwarded to immigration court. Hoping to err on the side of caution, officers refer more than 9 out of 10 asylum seekers in this manner.

If someone requests asylum, he or she may be placed in detention until the officer can schedule an interview. Some people are held at special immigration centers. Space is limited at these facilities, and when there is an overflow of applicants, they may be put in state and local prisons. Most asylum applicants are not placed in detention for long periods, but those few who find

Asian migrants are discovered by U.S. Coast Guardsmen in the cargo hold of a ship in the northern Hawaiian Islands, 1999. Stowing away in a ship or plane is a typical—though often dangerous—method of illegal migration.

themselves in such a situation experience several more months of fear and uncertainty about ever finding a safe haven.

The Asylum Interview

Once in the United States, threatened migrants who apply for asylum often need legal assistance to do it successfully. Lawyers can be expensive, but some social service groups and law firms will offer to help an asylum seeker for free.

After filing the application, the next step is an interview with an asylum officer. The purpose of the interview is to establish the facts, which are stated in the applicant's own words. The asylum officer determines whether applicants qualify for asylum. Applicants whose experiences involve nothing more severe than discrimination or harassment are rejected. In some cases, applicants are discovered to be former persecutors and are separated from the true victims.

In countries other than the United States, asylum seekers may have to wait in refugee camps until their applications are approved. This mother and child are waiting in a camp in northern France.

Many asylum applicants may speak no or very little English, which complicates the interview process. An interview will also include an interpreter if he or she is needed. A good interpreter will translate the questions and answers faithfully and accurately. But often, people speak at the same time. An asylum officer may interrupt an answer with another question, or vice versa. Important details can sometimes get lost in this situation.

Interviewing officers look for consistency in the applicant's story. The interview should establish exactly what happened. Does it match with the written testimony in the application? Substantial changes in the story may mean the applicant is not credible. The officer will closely examine any contradictions.

In developing the case's facts, the asylum officer seeks to determine whether the events of the applicant's story fall into one of the five grounds of persecution. The interviewer will ask direct questions like, "Why did the army or police choose you?" "Have you or your family done anything that would have attracted the attention of the authorities?" "Was everyone in the village treated badly by the guerillas when they arrived that night or did they single people out?" The answers to these questions help the asylum officer evaluate how the individual's fears match up against the legal grounds of granting asylum.

When they are available, written documents can sometimes help prove an asylum case, though many asylum seekers arrive with no papers at all. Some come prepared with statements from people who witnessed crucial events in their story. Medical reports can also be helpful, often illustrating unusual scarring or evidence of torture. (Of course, an X ray of a mended arm will not prove a prison guard broke it, but it can support the case better than no X ray at all.) Some applicants have seen a trauma counselor or psychologist, and the testimonies from these professionals can also persuade an interviewer one way or the other.

Groups like Amnesty International and Human Rights Watch often provide written reports of conditions in the applicant's home country. The officer examines these reports, as well as information from the Refugee Information Center (RIC). The RIC is the research branch of the Asylum Corps and provides general information on significant events as well as on a particular country or region. If an applicant's account contradicts this information, the officer will ask the right questions to set the record straight.

Asylum Officers and Asylum Hearings

Asylum officers are specially trained to speak with asylees. They study the culture of various high-refugee areas and develop approaches to cross-cultural communication. Many officers aim to have a professional yet sensitive reaction to the kinds of trauma that refugees describe. An asylum officer deals with high-stress situations, knowing that misinformed decisions can send applicants back into an environment where they face persecution, torture, and death.

Even worse, similar results can occur if the officer denies an asylum claim for legitimate reasons. There will inevitably be people who will be put in danger if they are deported, even if they didn't qualify for asylum. Some countries are so torn apart by violence that they are dangerous for the majority of the population. But if an applicant hasn't been personally singled out for mistreatment, he or she is not being persecuted. And without the personal nature of the violence, or threat of violence, an asylum officer has no choice but to deny a claim—even if it means possibly sending someone into danger.

On average, between 1992 and 2002 the Asylum Corps has approved approximately 30 percent of the cases they have heard, according to the 2002 *Yearbook of Immigration Statistics*. The many cases that aren't approved are referred to a hearing before an immigration judge. In cases in which people are in custody and look to avoid deportation, an immigration judge will also preside.

Unlike the asylum interview, the hearing is more like a standard court case. A lawyer defends the applicant's claim, while a BCIS attorney argues the case for deportation. The applicant is first questioned by his or her lawyer, and then is cross-examined by the BCIS attorney. Judges tend to put a lot of emphasis on how well an applicant's testimony holds up under cross-examination, and may ask for physical evidence to back up that testimony. This is generally a more difficult ordeal for the applicant, especially since some believe that immigration judges are more skeptical about asylum applicants.

7 LIFE IN THE NEW WORLD

The United States is challenging in every way. People speak a different language. A lot of food comes in plastic packages, and much of it is unhealthy. All consumers are faced with thousands of choices, and there are risky temptations, such as the immediate buying power offered by credit cards.

While asylees are adjusting to life in the United States, they are also coping with shattered lives. Loved ones are either dead or worlds removed from the United States. During the months—in some cases, years—before finding protection, asylees saw and did things they might have managed to briefly forget. But once they finally reach relative safety, those thoughts and fears return. People may suffer from recurring nightmares, or become clinically depressed.

Asylees typically go through similar psychological states, regardless of where they have come from. Initially, they go through a brief period of euphoria. Life in the United States is strange and new, but it feels safe, and the process of settling in requires too much attention to stop and dwell on the horrors of the past.

Soon, however, this new life proves to be not as easy as it first seemed. Many asylees fall into a deep depression. Their loss sinks in—they have lost friends, husbands, wives, or children, and they may never see their homeland again. As they finally start to cope with their loss, pressures from their new

◀ Cuban newcomers share stories at the counter of a restaurant in Miami, Florida. Asylees often look to their own ethnic community for support during the difficult period of adjustment in their new country.

life close in. They might have figured out the basics of their new country, but there is still a lot they don't understand.

Making it through this period is difficult. But after spending a few years in the United States, most people have begun rebuilding their lives. They have made friends, and put down some tentative roots in their new country. The feelings of loss remain, yet many asylees have found a way to cope.

Potential Problems

Certain aspects of living in the United States may place strains on asylee families. Different forces can draw the family apart. Parents typically work long hours for low pay, which will put food on the table but may put distance between children and parents.

Many asylee men and women often have trouble adjusting to gender role differences in American society. Women may have more responsibilities and freedoms in the home and the workplace than men are accustomed to. Power also can shift between the old and young. When children pick up English faster than their parents, they can slowly become the "family

Demanding labor, like the cigar rolling performed by this Cuban living in Miami, can often put a strain on immigrant families by removing parents from their children for long hours.

translator." During early stages of resettlement, the children's grasp of English can be very useful, but it can ultimately threaten the family structure. In having control over the information, the children can acquire more power than is customary. If the parents fall behind their children in English proficiency, conflicts can arise between generations.

Success and Service

Despite the obstacles asylees face, it is impossible to discount their spirit. The same fortitude they used to pull themselves out of their country can be used in making a new life. Some eventually pull the resources together to open their own businesses.

The booming U.S. economy during the late 1990s provided opportunities for many asylees. Some were able to buy homes within two years of arrival. They looked in areas with low housing costs and took advantage of government loans available to low-income buyers. Many asylees with regular jobs were able to make regular payments on loans and build good credit ratings. Although they may only have had one or two years of a legitimate financial history, this was often enough for some banks to hand out loans. Some asylees received loans even before they received permanent resident status.

A number of asylees have become politically active, working for human rights causes, or documenting war crimes in their homeland. Performing this kind of work has been rewarding for many refugees and asylees and has helped them maintain their connection to their homeland.

8 AFTER SEPTEMBER 11TH

On September 11, 2001, terrorists hijacked four passenger airplanes and used them to attack thousands of innocent civilians. Two planes flew into and destroyed the twin towers of the World Trade Center in New York City. One flew into the Pentagon in Washington, D.C. Passengers briefly regained control of the fourth plane, after which it crashed in rural Pennsylvania.

These attacks were executed and coordinated by foreign nationals. Most of them had entered the United States legally. Somehow, the U.S. immigration system allowed 19 terrorists into the country. There was no reason to believe that there were not more terrorists. Plugging the security holes in the immigration system became the new priority for the U.S. government.

Since the attacks, there have been several changes to the asylum system, which have resulted in a more restrictive asylum policy. Much of this policy stems from a renewed emphasis on security. With the intention of better protecting the country from another terrorist attack, the government erected new barriers for people asking for its protection.

A New Asylum System

The events of September 2001 brought about some significant changes in immigration policy that directly affect asylum seekers. Previously, the INS was in charge of almost all aspects

◀ A recovery worker surveys the debris of the World Trade Center in March 2002, six months after terrorists brought down the center's twin towers with hijacked airplanes. The 19 terrorists involved in the 2001 attacks had entered the United States on legal temporary visas.

of immigration service and enforcement. Today, the Bureau of Customs and Border Protection (BCBP) is in charge of admissions inspections at borders and airports. BCBP agents are the first officials that many asylum seekers will see upon arriving in the United States.

If an immigrant is deemed to have a credible fear after an interview with an asylum officer, he or she will be moved into the custody of the Bureau of Immigration and Customs Enforcement (BICE). Individuals will be held in a detention center (formerly run by the INS, now by the BICE) until a full asylum interview is scheduled.

Under the Homeland Security Act of 2002, refugee and asylum cases of unaccompanied minor children are now initially handled by the Department of Health and Human Services (HHS). Human rights groups had pushed for this change for years. They believed the HHS is better equipped to handle the needs of minors than either the new agencies or the former

A woman at the disaster site of the World Trade Center observes a moment of silence to mark the six-month anniversary of the terrorist attacks, March 2002. Since the attacks, some Americans have changed their attitudes toward asylum and immigration policy.

INS. However, Health and Human Services only decides where to place a juvenile while his or her case is being decided. It will not decide whether the juvenile is allowed to stay in the United States.

Another new development was the "safe third country" agreement signed by the United States and Canada in December 2002. In most cases, asylum seekers in the United States are now rejected if they first passed through Canada, and vice versa. This policy is intended to prevent people from seeking asylum in one country after they have been denied it in the other. Ironically, the policy is expected to increase the number of asylum applications in the United States, since most asylees have historically traveled there first before attempting entry into Canada.

These changes are new, and it is impossible to tell for certain how they will eventually play out. Still, the September 2001 terrorist attacks have eroded some of the American people's trust of outsiders, and these security-minded reforms reflect that distrust. Many would argue that in times of trouble, the idea of "protecting your own" is a natural impulse. But if the United States turns its back on asylum seekers, it would also turn its back on its heritage as a refuge for those fleeing political and religious persecution.

The identities of people who receive asylum are generally kept private, in accordance with U.S. law. Only when an asylee waives his or her right to privacy do others know that he or she has received asylum. Nonetheless, there have been some famous asylum cases, and some instances where even famous people were granted asylum.

One well-known account in 1945 is an asylum case that predates the era of granting official asylum. The persecuted party was Wernher von Braun, one of Germany's leading rocket engineers. He had designed the V-2 rockets that Germany used in World War II in the fall of 1944. Von Braun was more interested in using rockets for space exploration than as destructive weapons. The Nazi secret police, called the Gestapo, was aware of von Braun's preference and arrested him for crimes against the state. Essentially, he was charged with wasting his mental energy on space exploration when he was supposed to be building bigger missiles.

Von Braun's partner, Walter Dornberger, convinced the Gestapo that it should not keep von Braun interred, and he was released. Soon afterward, von Braun gathered his staff and held a meeting. They collectively agreed to surrender to U.S. forces. Using forged papers, the engineers stole a train to reach the American front, where they encountered an American private and surrendered to him.

In June 1945, Secretary of State Edward R. Stettinius agreed

◀ Ballet dancers Mikhail Baryshnikov (right) and Rudolf Nureyev, who died in 1993, both defected from the former Soviet Union and were granted asylum. In addition to being internationally known performers, they found success acting in Hollywood films.

to let von Braun and his remaining engineers immigrate to the United States. However, their migration would be kept confidential. As part of Operation Paperclip, each approved transfer was secretly marked with a paperclip atop the file. Von Braun and 126 other Germans were eventually transferred to the United States.

Whether or not von Braun and the others would qualify as asylees under today's laws and procedures is hard to say, but their skills did prove to be valuable contributions to the United States. They instructed U.S. soldiers on how to detect and avoid a rocket attack.

Von Braun, who was granted citizenship in 1955, continued his rocketry research in the United States. His teams built the Jupiter-C and Pershing missiles for the army, and on January 31, 1958, von Braun's team launched the first U.S. satellite, *Explorer 1*. Von Braun later directed the Saturn rocket program, which helped launch American astronauts to the moon in 1969.

Operation Paperclip proved to the U.S. government that there was a strategic benefit to providing asylum for people like von

Dr. Wernher von Braun (1912–77), a German rocket scientist, gave himself up to U.S. forces during World War II. He received asylum, and shortly after becoming a U.S. citizen, led the project to launch the first U.S. satellite, *Explorer 1*, in January 1958.

Braun and his colleagues. During the cold war, the political act of granting asylum retained its strategic value. Many Western countries provided asylum for famous artists, entertainers, and athletes form communist countries. Celebrities helped put a face on asylum for the general public. Their defections also supported the view that the Soviet government was oppressive and totalitarian. After all, if the celebrated elite were persecuted, how much worse was it for the average person?

The Soviet Union

Russian dancer Rudolf Nureyev was one of those persecuted elite. As a Leningrad ballet student in the 1950s, he would not attend meetings of the communist youth group called the Komsomol. But Nureyev shined on the ballet stage, earning a role as a soloist for the Leningrad Kiro Ballet soon after he graduated in 1958. Three years later, he slipped away from his touring company (and its Soviet guards) in France, and requested asylum at an airport. After receiving asylum, Nureyev took the opportunity to travel around the world, dancing in *Swan Lake*, *The Nutcracker*, and *Lucifer*, for which he had the title role.

Two decades later, another Soviet dancer followed in Nureyev's footsteps. Mikhail Baryshnikov defected in 1974, during a dance tour in Toronto. He claimed that Soviet Union's repressive system denied artists the freedom of expression, and that he was not allowed to perform many contemporary pieces. The Canadian government decided to grant him asylum.

In the West, Baryshnikov became a member of the American Ballet Theatre, choreographing and dancing in *The Nutcracker* and *Don Quixote*. In addition to becoming one of the most recognized contemporary dancers, he starred in movies such as *That's Dancing!* and *White Nights*, in which he played a Russian dancer who receives asylum in the United States. Another Soviet defector was grandmaster chess player Viktor Korchnoi. During a 1976 chess tournament in Amsterdam, Korchnoi defected and was granted asylum in the Netherlands.

A Brave Escape

Each of these cases was, in some way, a public relations victory against communism. In contrast, the asylum granted to Fauziya Kassindja in 1996 was a victory for compassion.

Fauziya was a teenager when she fled Africa with the help of her sister and mother. She was the youngest daughter of a wealthy Muslim family in Togo. Her father was a progressive thinker, and sent his daughters to boarding school for a better education. He would not consider letting his daughters marry unless they truly loved their suitors. What's more, he would not let his daughters undergo the traditional *kakia* procedure. Sometimes called "female circumcision," *kakia* is a brutal ritual. It is a painful and sometimes fatal mutilation of a female's— usually a 15-year-old girl's—genital area.

While Fauziya was at boarding school, her father died. The power in the family passed on to Fauziya's uncle. He and his wife drove Fauziya's mother away and then claimed custody for Fauziya and her younger brother. More traditional in their child-raising approach, the aunt and uncle took Fauziya out of boarding school and made plans for her to marry a 45-year-old man who already had three wives. Fauziya resisted, but one day she was told marriage preparations would begin, and in two days, she would undergo the *kakia*.

Fauziya was terrified, but felt powerless to stop it. The night before the *kakia* ceremony, her older sister helped her escape. Giving her money their mother had saved, Fauziya's sister led her into Ghana, where she arranged for a smuggler to get Fauziya on a flight to Germany. Once she was past German customs, she was on her own.

A kindhearted woman took Fauziya in, and eventually she made another friend who suggested that she apply for asylum. Since Fauziya spoke English but no German, the friend arranged for her to apply in the United States. Fauziya touched down at the airport on December 17, 1994. She asked for asylum almost immediately. However, when she told her story to the officer interviewing her, she left out details of the *kakia*. Fauziya was modest, and the story was too personal to relate.

Consequently, the initial report said that Fauziya left her country because she didn't want to marry the man her aunt had picked out, which was hardly worthy of asylum. Instead of receiving asylum, she endured 16 months in an INS detention center. Eventually, she made contact with law student Layli Miller Bashir and attorney Karen Musalo. They agreed to represent Fauziya in immigration court, where they fought a long legal battle to get her asylum.

The key was getting *kakia* recognized as a form of persecution. One important step was replacing the euphemism "female

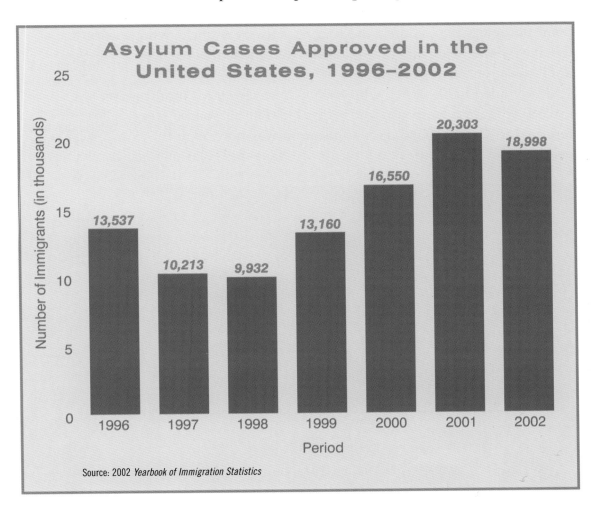

circumcision," which sounded medical and thus gave it false credibility. Bashir and Musalo worked to replace the term with the more explicit "female genital mutilation." FGM was eventually recognized as a form of persecution, grounds under which Fauziya could receive asylum. With this court victory, one immigrant had helped changed the asylum system.

The Debate over Elián

Another groundbreaking asylum case was that of Elián González. In November 1999, six-year-old Elián was rescued at sea off the coast of Florida. His mother had brought him with her as she fled Cuba. Their ship capsized and Elián's mother drowned, but he survived and was picked up by a fisherman. Soon Elián was paroled into the country. His great-uncle, who lived in Miami, claimed custody of him and filed an asylum application on Elián's behalf.

Meanwhile Elián's father, who was divorced from his mother, learned what had happened and requested that his son be returned to Cuba. The asylum application was now open to debate. Who should speak on behalf of Elián—his great uncle

In January 2000, a Cuban activist group demonstrates outside the home of Elián González' relatives in Miami, calling on the U.S. government to let the six-year-old boy remain in the United States. Thousands of Cuban Americans voiced their support for Elián, but in April 2000 U.S. courts turned down the boy's asylum application and ordered that he be returned to Cuba with his father.

in the United States, or his father in Cuba? Elián said he wanted to stay in the United States, but it hadn't been established yet if a child could apply for asylum against his parents' wishes. The legal battle over Elián moved from court to court.

On the morning of April 23, Justice Department agents stormed the home of Elian's uncle. Armed agents took Elián from his relatives and returned him to his father. In June, the U.S. Supreme Court refused to overturn a circuit court ruling against the relatives, ending the case. Elián and his father returned home to Cuba.

The World-Trotting Cyclist

Another asylum case that garnered news attention is that of Reza Baluchi, an Iranian national who has devoted himself to bicycling around the world to promote peace. He had been a member of Iran's bicycling team and served his required term in the military. Baluchi began to attend some unrecognized political meetings in his country, for which he was arrested and tortured. After several more arrests, one of which led to a one-and-a-half year stint in prison ending in 1996, Baluchi decided to leave the country.

He left on his bicycle, and for seven years pedaled almost all over the world. On November 10, 2002, Baluchi was picked up by U.S. Border Patrol agents. He had mistakenly ridden his bike across the U.S.–Mexico border while waiting for his U.S. visa to be approved. He had plans to ride to the World Trade Center memorial site in New York City, arriving on September 11, 2003, the second anniversary of the terrorist attacks.

Baluchi was detained for five months while his case was decided. He ran in the prison yard to keep in shape for his upcoming ride. While he was detained he promised that after he was released he would finish the peace tour on foot, running from Los Angeles to New York. In February 2003, Baluchi's asylum was approved, and as promised, he left Los Angeles in May, ran approximately 30 to 40 miles a day, and arrived in New York on September 11.

In 2003 Iranian exile Reza Baluchi completed a coast-to-coast journey across the United States on foot, running for the sake of world peace. After he was detained for five months as an undocumented immigrant, Baluchi received asylum and between May and September ran from Los Angeles to New York City for a total of 3,700 miles.

Cuban Baseball Players

Of course, not every asylum applicant is accepted, and not every celebrity defector becomes an asylee. In the summer of 2000, two Cuban baseball players—Andy Morales and Carlos Borrego—were discovered with 29 others aboard a smuggling ship headed to the United States. The ship had run out of gas, and its passengers tried to buy fuel from a passing boat. Instead of giving them fuel, the boat's captain radioed the Coast Guard.

Neither Morales nor Borrego established the "credible fear" that would have merited an asylum interview. All of the boat's passengers were turned back to Cuba. Other Cuban baseball players have been granted asylum in the United States, but Morales was the first high-profile Cuban star to be rejected.

There are sure to be more famous asylum cases in the future. But for every asylum case that makes the news, there are thousands more that do not, and there is as much at stake in an anonymous case as there is in the most public: liberty, the pursuit of happiness, and, quite possibly, someone's life.

GLOSSARY

affirmative application—an asylum application filed before a deportation order has been issued.

anti-Semitic—pertaining to the persecution of Jews.

asylee—an alien in the United States who receives asylum, meeting the legal definition of an individual who is unable or unwilling to return to his or her home country due to a fear of persecution on account of race, religion, nationality, political opinion, or particular social group.

asylum—protection granted by a government to a refugee from another country.

defensive application—an asylum application filed as a defense against a deportation order.

deportation—the formal removal of an alien by the United States after he or she has broken immigration laws.

expedited removal—the immediate removal from the United States of an alien found to be lacking valid entry documents at a port of entry.

internally displaced—the state of being forced from one's home but still in the country of origin.

lawful permanent resident—a non-citizen legally residing in the United States.

lobby—an organized attempt to convince a legislator to vote a certain way on an issue.

naturalization—the process of becoming a citizen.

parole—a process in which the Secretary of Homeland Security can legally admit a group of aliens into the United States.

persecution—the infliction of suffering or harm on a group because of their ethnic origins or beliefs.

refoulement—the forced return of a refugee to his or her country of origin.

refugee—an alien outside the United States who is unable or unwilling to return to his or her country of nationality because of persecution or a well-founded fear of persecution.

repatriation—the voluntary return of a refugee to his or her country of origin.

resettlement—the permanent relocation of refugees in a place outside their country of origin.

restrictionist—one who wants much stricter limits on immigration to the United States.

visa—an official authorization that permits arrival at a port of entry but does not guarantee admission into the United States.

FURTHER READING

Bahrampour, Tara. *To See and See Again: A Life in Iran and America*. New York: Farrar, Strauss, and Giroux, 1999.

Castles, Stephen, and Mark J. Miller. *The Age of Migration*, 2nd ed. New York: The Guilford Press, 1998.

Einolf, Christopher J. *The Mercy Factory: Refugees and the American Asylum System*. Chicago, Ill.: Ivan R. Dee, 2001.

Gonzalez-Pando, Miguel. *The Cuban Americans*. Westport, Conn.: Greenwood Press, 1998.

Kassindja, Fauziya, and Layli Miller Bashir. *Do They Hear You When You Cry*. New York: Delacorte Press, 1998.

Laguerre, Michel S. *Haitian Americans in Transnational America*. New York: St. Martin's Press, 1998.

Lee, Kathleen. *Illegal Immigration*. San Diego, Calif.: Lucent Books, 1996.

Little, Allan, and Laura Silber. *Yugoslavia: Death of a Nation*. New York: n Books, 1997.

Loescher,   d John A. Scanlan. *Calculated Kindness*. New York: The Free Press, 1986.

McClellan, Grant S., ed. *Immigrants, Refugees, and U.S. Policy.* New York: H. W. Wilson Company, 1981.

Pipher, Mary. *The Middle of Everywhere: The World's Refugees Come to Our Town*. New York: Harcourt, 2002.

FURTHER READING

Schrag, Philip G. *A Well-Founded Fear: The Congressional Battle to Save Political Asylum in America*. New York: Routledge, 2000.

Shawcross, William. *The Quality of Mercy*. New York: Simon and Schuster, 1984.

Suleiman, Michael W., ed. *Arabs in America: Building a New Future*. Philadelphia: Temple University Press, 1999.

United Nations High Commissioner for Refugees. *The State of the World's Refugees*. Oxford: Oxford University Press, 2000.

Zucker, Norman L., and Naomi Flink Zucker. *Desperate Crossings: Seeking Refuge in America*. Armonk, N.Y.: M.E. Sharpe, 1996.

INTERNET RESOURCES

http://www.bcis.gov

The website of the Bureau of Citizenship and Immigration services explains the various functions of the organization and provides specific information on immigration policy.

http://www.canadianhistory.ca/iv/main.html

This site contains an excellent history of immigration to Canada from the 1800s to the present.

http://www.hrw.org/refugees

The home site of Human Rights Watch is an up-to-date resource covering refugee issues and the recent campaigns of advocacy groups.

http://www.irb.gc.ca

The page for the Immigration and Refugee Board, Canada, provides descriptions of the board's different programs, as well as instructions on how to apply for asylum in Canada.

http://www.refugees.org

The website of the U.S. Committee for Refugees covers refugee issues involving the United States and provides updates on the most recent developments of the committee.

http://www.interaction.org/refugees

This page of the American Council for Voluntary International Action reports on the latest developments of its refugee assistance program, which is one of many operations serving the organization's agenda of social justice.

Internet Resources

http://www.worldrefugee.com

This website of the WorldNews Network is a source for the latest news on refugees.

http://www.lchr.org

The home site of the Lawyers Committee for Human Rights is an informative source, covering the organization's efforts to support refugees and other victims of persecution or repression.

http://www.unhcr.ch/cgi-bin/texis/vtx/home

The official site of the United Nations High Commissioner for Refugees gives updates on developments worldwide and providing opportunities to donate to refugee causes.

INDEX

Numbers in ***bold italic*** refer to captions.

INDEX

SENATOR EDWARD M. KENNEDY has represented Massachusetts in the United States Senate for more than forty years. Kennedy serves on the Senate Judiciary Committee, where he is the senior Democrat on the Immigration Subcommittee. He currently is the ranking member on the Health, Education, Labor and Pensions Committee in the Senate, and also serves on the Armed Services Committee, where he is a member of the Senate Arms Control Observer Group. He is also a member of the Congressional Friends of Ireland and a trustee of the John F. Kennedy Center for the Performing Arts in Washington, D.C.

Throughout his career, Kennedy has fought for issues that benefit the citizens of Massachusetts and the nation, including the effort to bring quality health care to every American, education reform, raising the minimum wage, defending the rights of workers and their families, strengthening the civil rights laws, assisting individuals with disabilities, fighting for cleaner water and cleaner air, and protecting and strengthening Social Security and Medicare for senior citizens.

Kennedy is the youngest of nine children of Joseph P. and Rose Fitzgerald Kennedy, and is a graduate of Harvard University and the University of Virginia Law School. His home is in Hyannis Port, Massachusetts, where he lives with his wife, Victoria Reggie Kennedy, and children, Curran and Caroline. He also has three grown children, Kara, Edward Jr., and Patrick, and four grandchildren.

Senior consulting editor STUART ANDERSON served as Executive Associate Commissioner for Policy and Planning and Counselor to the Commissioner at the Immigration and Naturalization Service from August 2001 until January 2003. He spent four and a half years on Capitol Hill on the Senate Immigration Subcommittee, first for Senator Spencer Abraham and then as Staff Director of the subcommittee for Senator Sam Brownback. Prior to that, he was Director of Trade and Immigration Studies at the Cato Institute in Washington, D.C., where he produced reports on the history of immigrants in the military and the role of immigrants in high technology. He currently serves as Executive Director of the National Foundation for American Policy, a nonpartisan public policy research organization focused on trade, immigration, and international relations. He has an M.A. from Georgetown University and a B.A. in Political Science from Drew University. His articles have appeared in such publications as the *Wall Street Journal*, *New York Times*, and *Los Angeles Times*.

MARIAN L. SMITH served as the senior historian of the U.S. Immigration and Naturalization Service (INS) from 1988 to 2003, and is currently the immigration and naturalization historian within the Department of Homeland Security in Washington, D.C. She studies, publishes, and speaks on the history of the immigration agency and is active in management of official 20th-century immigration records.

PETER HAMMERSCHMIDT is the First Secretary (Financial and Military Affairs) for the Permanent Mission of Canada to the United Nations. Before taking this position, he was a ministerial speechwriter and policy specialist for the Department of National

Defence in Ottawa. Prior to joining the public service, he served as the Publications Director for the Canadian Institute of Strategic Studies in Toronto. He has a B.A. (Honours) in Political Studies from Queen's University, and an MScEcon in Strategic Studies from the University of Wales, Aberystwyth. He currently lives in New York, where in his spare time he operates a freelance editing and writing service, Wordschmidt Communications.

Manuscript reviewer ESTHER OLAVARRIA serves as General Counsel to Senator Edward M. Kennedy, ranking Democrat on the U.S. Senate Judiciary Committee, Subcommittee on Immigration. She is Senator Kennedy's primary advisor on immigration, nationality, and refugee legislation and policies. Prior to her current job, she practiced immigration law in Miami, Florida, working at several non-profit organizations. She cofounded the Florida Immigrant Advocacy Center and served as managing attorney, supervising the direct service work of the organization and assisting in the advocacy work. She also worked at Legal Services of Greater Miami, as the directing attorney of the American Immigration Lawyers Association Pro Bono Project, and at the Haitian Refugee Center, as a staff attorney. She clerked for a Florida state appellate court after graduating from the University of Florida Law School. She was born in Havana, Cuba, and raised in Florida.

Reviewer JANICE V. KAGUYUTAN is Senator Edward M. Kennedy's advisor on immigration, nationality, and refugee legislation and policies. Prior to working on Capitol Hill, Ms. Kaguyutan was a staff attorney at the NOW Legal Defense and Education Fund's Immigrant Women Program. Ms. Kaguyutan has written and trained extensively on the rights of immigrant victims of domestic violence, sexual assault, and human trafficking. Her previous work includes representing battered immigrant women in civil protection order, child support, divorce, and custody hearings, as well as representing immigrants before the Immigration and Naturalization Service on a variety of immigration matters.

ROB STAEGER lives and writes in New Jersey. He has written dozens of short stories for children, and even more newspaper stories for adults. He has also written 10 books, including *Wyatt Earp*, *Native American Tools and Weapons*, and *The Journey of Lewis and Clark*. This book is once again dedicated to his father, without whom he couldn't have done it.

PICTURE CREDITS